VINTAGE ROGER

Vintage Roger

Letters from the POW Years

Roger Mortimer

Edited by Charlie Mortimer

CONSTABLE

Contents

Introduction

My father would have been more than a little astonished to learn that, over twenty years after his death, his letters written to me in my rackety youth had become a best-selling book in the form of *Dear Lupin,* and a West End play. Nevertheless, I think what might have surprised him more than anything else is that, despite living out of a suitcase for many years, I had somehow managed to hang on to the letters. One can only then imagine his reaction to find that the letters he had written as POW No. 481, from various Oflags and Stalags during World War II, to his friend Peggy Dunne had been kept by her and her family and now, some eighty years later, were to be shared with a rather larger audience. These seventy or so letters and postcards form the core of this book.

My father's role as an active combatant in the last war was short-lived. Roger Mortimer was born in 1909, educated at Ludgrove (then called Wixenford), Eton and RMC Sandhurst. In 1930, he was commissioned into the

3rd Battalion Coldstream Guards and for the following years enjoyed a fairly leisurely existence stationed at Chelsea Barracks, barely five minutes' walk from his parents' house in Cadogan Square. Official military duties beyond drill practice were minimal by today's standards and much time was spent on the racecourse, in the hunting field or enjoying London's clubs and nightlife. Each officer was allocated a 'soldier servant' who took care of his personal requirements and could look forward to twenty or so weeks' annual leave as well as most weekends off.

In the spring of 1938, now a captain, my father sailed with the 3rd Battalion CG for their Palestine tour during the 'Arab Uprising', a posting that, by all accounts, he hugely enjoyed. Shortly after the outbreak of war with Germany in September 1939 he was dispatched with the 1st Battalion CG as part of the British Expeditionary Force in Northern France and Belgium, in what was initially called the 'phoney war'. Some months later he found himself fighting a desperate rearguard action against the German advance on the Dyle river in Belgium. A shell exploded nearby and he was knocked unconscious and left for dead.

At the time he was incorrectly reported by the authorities to have been killed in action. When he came to later he found himself surrounded by German soldiers; recounted here in my father's classic understated style: 'A fairly unpleasant German officer told me I was to be shot immediately because "the dirty British had been using poisoned gas". Fortunately, that little difficulty blew over.' Now officially a prisoner of war (POW or, in German slang, *Kreigie*), as POW No. 481 he was destined to endure the status for the next five long and challenging years.

At my father's thanksgiving service in 1992 his close friend and fellow Coldstreamer, Brigadier Raoul Lempriere-Robin, observed, 'I always feel it is quite out of keeping for anyone who has not himself been a prisoner of war to expound upon the realities and consequences of life as such.' My father's letters from that time offer a unique and interesting insight into the harsh and complicated realities of being a POW during a seemingly endless period of incarceration with an unknown end-date.

In a letter written shortly after he was captured he said, 'I suppose after thirty years of ease, a little discomfort is good for one but I hate never having a bath and having only one set of clothes.' Adjusting to life as a prisoner required any number of qualities, such as courage, resilience and resourcefulness, together with less obvious ones, including tolerance, good manners and, probably the most important of all, friendship combined with loyalty. In later life, the vast majority of my father's closest friends were those he knew as a prisoner. As I grew up, I got to know them almost as if they were family, and I look back on them and their mutual, understated strength of character, sense of fun and generosity of spirit with huge affection.

The regular letters from Peggy were an absolute lifeline for him. Correspondence with an entertaining friend is rather different than that with family members and there was nothing my father enjoyed more than an appreciative audience (like father, like son!): 'Quite honestly I should feel very lost without your letters now, you are about the only person I hear from whose letters aren't a series of drab commonplace mixed up with a few sops in the shape of foolish optimism. I've been told "next Christmas" since

3

August 1940. As long as you can stand it please go on – until you've been in prison you can't possibly realise what letters mean.'

Understandably, there were times as a POW when things seemed particularly desolate. In June 1943, he wrote to his own father, 'This has been a wretched month. Today, to crown everything, most of my room have been moved to another camp, including Freddy Corfield whom I've lived with for over three years in quiet content and a considerable amount of laughter. What sanity I still possess is largely due to him. Friendship is about the only anchor one has in prison and now after three years I feel just as if I was starting all over again. I suppose my resistance to the bleakness of things is decreasing, but at present I feel like attaching my old school braces to the lamp bracket, fitting a snug knot behind my ears and jumping off the table.'

Apart from being great friends, for several years Fred and my father had controlled the vital news flow from their concealed radio the 'Canary Bird' (see note below). And, fortunately, life wasn't always as gloomy, as in a letter home later that year: 'Lovely room here. I am wearing a nice heather mixture tie, knitted for me by Francis Reed out of an old sock.'

Sometimes the benefit of hindsight reduces somewhat the frisson of the realities of a given situation as it was at the time. For my father as a POW it seemed highly unlikely that the allied forces would ultimately be victorious, as he observed in 1942. 'Apparently we are relying on entirely two neutrals – God and the USA –to win the war for us.'

One of my favourite extracts from his letters home is his response to a particularly pessimistic observation from his father, who at the time was living in some style at 28 Cadogan Square with ten permanent staff. 'I take that to be merely an instance of that astonishing capacity for looking on the bleakest side of every prospect which is such a feature of our family life and which I myself share to the full. Ever since I can remember we've always been hovering on the edge of a bed-sitting room in the Cromwell Road, but by tremendous good fortune we never quite seem to get there.'

It is often said that the war shaped my father's generation, as a friend recently confided to me, in that 'they weren't so much hardened by the war as realised that nothing that bad could happen in normal life. So it produced that toughness, lack of self-pity and self-regard.'

In 'Fifty Years On' my father gives a typically light-hearted account of leaving RMC Sandhurst in 1929 and being commissioned into the 3rd Battalion Coldstream Guards and describes the way that, for the following nine or so years, he enjoyed a rather relaxed routine stationed at Chelsea Barracks. At the time it was the habit for officers in the Coldstream Guards to be given nicknames. My father's was 'Pol Roger' (see note below). All this was very different to his subsequent existence as prisoner of war No. 481.

The book concludes with a lengthy and utterly charming personal letter to me, diarising a period of some seventeen years between 1949 and 1967 with all the difficulties both enjoyed and endured at Barclay House, our family home in Hampshire. For me, this is a celebration of those rather austere post-war years, when the simple pleasures of life were, after all that had gone before, to be enjoyed to the full. My father writes very much in the style so admired and enjoyed in *Dear Lupin* and *Dear Lumpy* and, as in those books, it is my father's voice that is heard rather than that of his editor – in this case, his son.

My father was a very modest man and his subsequent success as a racing journalist and author came not through calculated manipulation and jostling for position but through being very good at what he did. Above all, irrelevant of circumstances, it was his humour, intelligence and decency combined with a quiet acceptance of the status quo that tended to shine and get him through. If my father had a secret weapon it was his self-deprecating humour that ridiculed inflated egos and somehow made the unendurable more endurable. If I have inherited anything from my father, I like to think it's his gallows humour.

In conclusion, and in his own words as said to me on numerous occasions, 'There was never a time as a prisoner of war that was quite as bad as the first term at my preparatory school.'

The Canary Bird

In February 1941, while in the prison at Spangenburg castle, my father and fellow POW and friend Fred Corfield managed to acquire a tiny radio set about ten inches by four inches – it was this device that was nicknamed the Canary Bird – from a party of doctors who had brought it into the camp undetected in a medical case and were worried about the extremely severe consequences of it being found in their possession. As Fred remembers, 'Whether Roger and I took charge or whether we were elected to do so, I do not remember, and from then on, we took it in turns to take down the news virtually every night, only missing out when the radio was in transit from one camp to another,' cleverly concealed as it was in a medicine ball. A news distribution system was soon contrived so that everyone was informed of the latest world news – free from German propaganda. It cannot be overestimated what a massive boost to morale this was, in particular hearing extracts from Churchill's speeches. Given how hopelessly impractical my father was, running the radio with Fred was quite an achievement. There is however an apocryphal story that one afternoon my father blotted his copybook by 'blowing a valve' when listening to a live race broadcast from Newmarket.

'Pol Roger'

In the 1930s it was customary for officers in the Coldstream Guards to be given nicknames a step or two removed from their birth names. My father's was 'Pol Roger' (after the fizz) and thus 'Paul'. Hence the title of this book 'Vintage Roger'. Any reference in the letters by my father to Paul such as : 'Paul quite likes his new school, although the wartime regime is Spartan in the extreme. The masters are pretty strict...' is my father talking about his situation in the third party in an attempt to slip certain negative facts about his new camp past the German censors.

Dramatis Personae

PEGGY DUNNE (née Margaret Walker). Just a few years older than my father and the recipient of some seventy of his letters and postcards (around which this book is based) whilst he was on active service in Northern France (1940) and subsequently a POW (1940-45). Throughout his life my father loved engaging intellectually with bright and amusing women and, as in all his letters, he excelled at playing to his audience. In a letter to his father at Christmas 1941 he wrote, 'Could you sometime spare a second to ring up Peggy Dunne, who has written marvellous letters every single week since I've been in chokey, as well as sending scores of books?'

One or two mischievously minded people, such as my grandmother and the bossy matron at the hospital where Peggy was working, suggested they were having an unhealthy liaison by letter. I am absolutely certain that was not the case.

I know little more about Peggy and her life beyond the fact that she survived well into her nineties. She did, however, run an auxiliary hospital, in Warwickshire during the war.

Peggy married dashing Philip Dunne in April 1930 (dissolved by divorce in 1944); they had two sons, Thomas and Martin, and a daughter, Phillipa. Philip was later awarded an MC, remarried in 1945 and ultimately became a Tory MP. Regrettably, I have no idea if my father and Peggy ever met after the war.

RONALD (Ronnie) STRUTT (later 4th Baron Belper). One of my father's best and, in many ways, most challenging of friends. Born in 1912, he was educated at Harrow and RMC Sandhurst. He was commissioned into the Coldstream Guards a couple of years after my father and also stationed at Chelsea barracks. Very much a man's man, an excellent horseman (later master of the Quorn hunt), fearless, intensely loyal and kind to his friends, Ronnie and my father shared many interests – horse-racing, fox-hunting and the company of women from all walks of life among them. Both enjoyed some success as amateur jockeys, Ronnie winning the National Hunt Challenge Cup at Cheltenham in 1934. Ronnie and his sister Lavinia, later Duchess of Norfolk, were among the most noted equestrians of their generation.

Ronnie enjoyed being perverse and was definitely not a man to be trifled with. I am not sure that he and my father were particularly good influences on each other – I well remember my father relating how, not entirely sober, they went to Bertram Mills Circus in Olympia in the early 1930s. In a sideshow they came across an Indian snake charmer who was performing all sorts of tricks with a huge python. I gather the man was persuaded to coil the snake around his neck by Ronnie, in return for a guinea. Ronnie then stuck the snake sharply on its head with his ivory-handled umbrella, leaving the hapless snake-charmer literally fighting for his life. I can quite see why Ronnie wasn't one of my mother's favourites in later years.

Ronnie is mentioned many, many times in these letters and it becomes clear that, not being much of a letter writer himself, he had somehow managed to persuade his close friend Peggy to write to Roger – at the time fighting with the British Expeditionary Force in northern France – in his place. That was how this unlikely correspondence was established. Peggy sent my father well over a hundred letters, as well as many entertaining books and gramophone records, between 1940 and 1945, during which time Ronnie managed to write just the one letter.

The three of them had numerous friends in common and in the five years covered by their correspondence, Ronnie managed to live life to the full – marrying Zara Mainwaring in 1940, producing son and heir Richard in 1941 and seeing vigorous active service as a captain until wounded in 1944. With their shared love of racing, Ronnie's friendship with my father fully resumed after the war and continued up to his death in 1991. Ronnie died in 1999, aged eighty-seven.

Immediate Family

HALIBURTON STANLEY MORTIMER. My grandfather. A lovely man once described as the worst stockbroker in London, much happier in his London club or on the golf course.

DOROTHY MORTIMER (née Blackwell, of Crosse & Blackwell). My grandmother. There is an apocryphal story that her first letter to my father as a POW started, 'Trust you to get captured', and when, having been liberated, he returned home some five years later she was annoyed that his surprise arrival had upset the staff's routine.

JOAN MORTIMER. My aunt – 'One of life's eternal girl guides'. Among other achievements, she taught the Queen how to swim. Somewhat against the odds, in later life, she married delightful barrister Reggie Cockburn.

In order of appearance

MAJOR F. G. CHALMERS. My father's company commander at RMC Sandhurst said to favour Etonians and cadets who hunted.

FRANK FURLONG. Contemporary at RMC Sandhurst, as was the famous trainer FULKE WALWYN. Both rode Reyoldsdown to victory in the Grand National. Furlong in 1935 and Walwyn in 1936. Furlong was subsequently killed flying in action.

LT. COL. ALBERT PAINE. My grandfather's old commanding officer. 'For God's sake don't ask me. I'm the last person to know what's going on.'

GENERAL SIR CAMERON SHUTE. A keen inspector of latrines nicknamed 'Deus ex latrina'.

CAPTAIN HORNTON. Aka 'Browndog', Hornton was unimpressed by my father's attempts to sing the 'Sevenfold Amen'.

JOHN HUNT. High-minded contemporary at Royal Military College (RMC) Sandhurst, who later led the 1953 expedition that conquered Mount Everest. He was subsequently knighted for that achievement.

KEN DARLING. My uncle. Contemporary at RMC Sandhurst, later General Sir Kenneth Darling, whose obituary read, 'He terrorised the terrorists.' He married my mother's older sister, Pamela Denison-Pender.

DAVID NIVEN. The actor. Contemporary at RMC Sandhurst, my father once observed that he was the most insincere person he had ever met.

CAPTAIN 'BOY' BROWNING of the Grenadiers and CAPTAIN MOORE of the Royal Inniskilling Fusiliers. Both successive adjutants at RMC Sandhurst.

REGIMENTAL SERGEANT MAJOR PEARSON. A Cold-streamer who held a certain distain for non-Guardsmen. 'Go on salute the adjutant (Capt. Moore) it's good practice.'

SERGEANT KER. Keen on poaching and betting.

SERGEANT BIRD. An equitation instructor with an original and highly entertaining turn of phrase.

OFFICER CADET HUGH JONES. A bit of a cad and an expert at 'pig sticking'. Did a bunk with his squadron commander's wife.

COLONEL WYLD. A well-connected ex-boyfriend of my grandmother's.

HERBERT SMITH. An amiable Epsom trainer with frank views.

OFFICER CADET HUGO BRASSEY. He possessed a keen sense of humour which tended to work to his disadvantage.

ARTHUR PILKINGTON. Joined 3rd Battalion Coldstream Guards at Chelsea barracks with my father in January 1930. There is a report, circa 3 May 1945, of Major Arthur Pilkington taking a 'patrol' into Hamburg to 'find wine' for the officers' mess and managing 'by accident' to officially 'liberate' the city!

ANGUS McCORQUODALE. Contemporary Coldstreamer. 'Corkers', picquet officer at Chelsea barracks. A delightful man, painfully shy and possessed of a keen sense of duty. Sadly killed when leading his company 'with great gallantry' in 1940.

My father's soldier servants: GUARDSMAN WRIGHT, later transformed somehow into L/Sgt Corporal MacDonald of the Scots Guards!; GUARDSMAN BIRCH, who remained in regular contact with my father for more than fifty years; GUARDSMAN (Charlie) BIRKS, a Yorkshireman with a big character and a dry sense of humour; GUARDSMAN LEE, a very kind man, sadly killed when my father was captured in May 1940.

Other outstanding soldier servants in the Coldstream Guards, both of whom were turf fanatics: GUARDSMAN CROOM, looked after Gerry Feilden, later General Sir Randle Feilden, member of the Jockey Club and in charge of horse-racing security; GUARDSMAN SKEDWELL, who looked after John Baillie, also later a member of the Jockey Club.

GEORGE PEREIRA. Fellow officer at Chelsea Barracks who was fond of a tipple!

JOHN LASCELLES. Fellow officer and talented card player. On night exercise he once famously observed, 'You might not think it to look at me now, boys, but I was had a good deal at Eton in my day.'

RONALD TRUE. Inmate of Broadmoor, found guilty of strangling a 'lady of the night' in the Fulham Road.

COLONEL RUTHERFORD. Inmate at Broadmoor, found guilty of shooting his second-in-command, whom he wrongly suspected of 'doing his wife'.

SERGEANT TOMBS. Heavily moustached gentleman who referred to everyone as 'this individual'; and SERGEANT FLINT who looked like a budgerigar. Both were weapons instructors at Chelsea barracks.

HEWITT and HAWKINS. The two charismatic waiters of very differing builds at the Guards' Club.

FLETCHER. Secretary of the Guards' Club. He used to get seriously sloshed and talk to himself. 'God, Fletcher, you are drunk tonight!'

WILLIE WALSH. Later Lord Ormthwaite, a kindly old boy and owner of Pratts' Club.

REGIMENTAL SERGEANT MAJOR 'TIPPER' DAVIS. Known for his colourful language on the parade ground.

DRILL SERGEANT PRINTER. Prone to exaggerate and possessed a good grasp of irony.

DRILL SERGEANT VICKERS. All three parade ground sergeants sported moustaches and all had fought with distinction in the Great War.

BANK-PICQUET KATE. Local eccentric.

JOHN HISLOP. Highly accomplished amateur jockey, journalist, author, racehorse breeder and member of the Jockey Club. Life-long friend of my father who, together with his larger-than-life wife, Jean, bred the great champion racehorse Brigadier Gerard. John who, among many other things, wrote the racing column for the *News of the World*, was small in stature whereas Jean, famous for her legendary Christmas parties, outrageous behaviour and colourful language, was of a somewhat larger build.

VICTOR GILPIN. Well-known Newmarket trainer.

ARTHUR FORTESCUE. Promoted to rank of brigadier and awarded MC and an MBE; RONALD DOUGLAS SPEED, sadly killed in action at Dunkirk; and TOMMY GORE-BROWNE – all fellow Coldstreamers with the British Expeditionary Force, 1940.

BEVERLEY NICHOLS. English author, playwright, composer

and journalist, was once rumoured to have had an affair with Siegfried Sassoon.

ERIC WYATT. Fellow Coldstreamer known as 'Pop' Wyatt. He was a qualified barrister, some five years older than my father and, as a major, was his senior. Despite being badly wounded at La Penne he refused to leave his men and subsequently very sadly died at Dunkirk.

SAM HOLDSWORTH. Letter-writing friend with a predilection for pornography and 'vivid powers of describing "certain subjects" in detail'.

HESTOR LLOYD. Contemporary debutante possessed of 'an acid wit'.

MADAME KOKO. Charismatic and canny Madame of a bordello in northern France.

DYEBEL. Thoroughbred racehorse.

MRS 'FLASH' KELLETT (née Helen Myrtle Dorothy Atherley). Mutual friend and very beautiful wife of Lieutenant Colonel Edward Orlando 'Flash' Kellett, who was killed in action in North Africa in 1943. She was ultimately awarded an MBE for services to soldiers' welfare.

CAPTAIN PHILIP DUNNE. Peggy's gallant husband.

'DEAR PETER' (Sir Peter Thorne). Later 33rd serjeant-at-arms in the House of Commons. He was the son of General 'Bulgy' Thorne.

GENERAL REICHENAU (*Generalfeldmarschall* Walter von Reichenau). 'How is "Bulgy" Thorne? I have not seen him since Ascot.' An aristocrat, enthusiastic Nazi and keen consumer of 'Turks Blood' – a half-and-half mixture of claret and champagne – ultimately died from a stroke.

GENERAL 'BULGY' THORNE (Andrew Thorne). Ex-Grenadier Guards, he explained, 'My nickname came from a dog whose fondness for buns was only equalled by mine. At the age of eight-and-a-half and on the dog's demise the name descended on me. I have never been able to escape it.'

GENERAL VON RUNSTEDT (*Generalfeldmarschall* Karl Rudolf Gerd von Runstedt). A highly decorated and much respected German officer in the Wehrmacht. My father guarded him when he was a prisoner after the war in Kensington Palace Gardens. 'He was far more agreeable and amusing than many senior British officers . . . I used to take him a drink in the evening and we enjoyed a good gossip together.'

JOHN SCOTT and JACK PRICE. Mutual friends on active service.

JACK DENNIS. Amorous friend.

JIM M. LEWIS. Very close friend.

GREENSLADE. Fellow POW in Stalag XX who did solitary for playing poker after lights out.

SOPHIE LYELL (née Trafford). Married Charles Antony Lyell, 2nd Baron Lyell. They had one son also named Charles. While serving as a captain in the Scots Guards in Tunisia in April 1943, her husband (known as Antony) was tragically killed in action and awarded a posthumous VC. Sophie was a close friend who also wrote to my father from time to time. In one letter home my father wrote, 'Please thank Sophie for her lovely libellous letter' and, in another following the death of her husband, 'I've written to Sophie but couldn't think of much to say. I hope she doesn't take Antony's death too hard.'

DAVID MITCHELL. My father's first cousin, tragically killed in action, aged only twenty, while serving as a second lieutenant in 1st Battalion Royal Fusiliers, in the battle for Keren as part of the East Africa campaign, on 16 March 1941.

ROSE FISKE. Friend.

MARCUS MARSH. POW in Oflax IX/A, served in the RAF. Hugely successful trainer both before and after the war. Notable classic wins included the Derby (twice) and St Leger (twice) with Windsor Lad in 1934 and Tulyar in 1952 as well as the 2000 Guineas with Palestine in 1950.

JOCK DELVES BROUGHTON. Tried and acquitted of murdering 'love rival' Josslyn Hay 22nd Earl of Erroll, in Kenya in 1941. A member of the infamous Happy Valley set. Subsequently took his own life at the Adelphi hotel, Liverpool, the following year.

NIGEL COURAGE (15th/19th King's Royal Hussars) and OSSY YOUNGER (Argyle and Sutherland Highlanders). Fellow and extremely stoic POWs in OFLAG IX A. Nigel Courage lost a leg at Dunkirk and Ossy Younger was more than partially blinded.

PHILIP MOORE. Friend of Sophie Lyell and fellow POW in OFLAG IX A, subsequently repatriated, having lost a leg at the thigh.

JOHN (DENZIL) FOX-STRANGWAYS. Fellow Coldstreamer, recently wounded.

RALPH COBBOLD (fellow Coldstreamer, POW in OFLAG VI/B and talented all-round sportsman), JACK FAUCUS (fellow POW in VI/B and excellent horseman), PETER DOLLAR (fellow POW in OFLAG VI/B, and a good friend of Peggy. Not really my father's 'cup of tea' it would appear!).

TIGER SUDELEY. Friend who had died recently.

RACHEL WILLOUGHBY. Old flame.

RICHARD WOOD (fellow POW in OFLAG VI/B, professional conductor and classical music buff), COLONEL DONALD FRASER (fellow POW in OFLAG VI/B commanded 16th Hussars). Benjamin Britten wrote a short work for male voices, *The Ballad of Little Musgrave and Lady Bernard*, and dedicated it to 'Richard Wood and the musicians of OFLAG VII B'. The piece was completed on 13 December 1943 and smuggled into the camp on microfilm for the POWs to sing.

PORTOBELLO. Successful thoroughbred racehorse born 1936, sired by Portlaw through Zingarella. Perhaps owned by Ronnie or Peggy?

CHARLIE HOPETOUN. Earl of Hopetoun, 1st Lothians and Border Yeomanry and POW at OFLAG VI/B. He was 'superb as ugly sister in camp pantomime' and as a contemporary put it, 'The life and soul of anything he put his mind to.' Subsequently moved to Colditz Castle and awarded an MC.

BOB LAYCOCK. Evelyn Waugh's commanding officer in World War II, 'said by many to have no enemies'. Later Major General Sir Robert Laycock. He was also Philip Dunne's commanding officer as well as a close friend. He subsequently married Ian Fleming's niece Lucy. Several years ago, I suggested my good friend and retired bank robber Dean bought as an investment a comprehensive set of Evelyn Waugh first editions, generously inscribed by him to Bob Laycock. It was only several years later when Dean came to sell them, at a handsome profit, he discovered, much to his surprise, that Evelyn wasn't a woman.

CAPTAIN JONES. Acquaintance who hunted with the Whaddon and whose general lifestyle attracted my father's displeasure. Unlike MAURICE KINGSCOTE who, it seems, 'made good'.

MILLY. A saucy friend. 'I like coarse jokes, Milly, and most tarts.'

NEVILLE USHER. Rather younger POW in OFLAG VI/B.

THE WELDON BROTHERS. Acquaintances who possessed a sense of entitlement and overbearing bonhomie that grated with my father.

DOUGLAS BADER. POW in OLFLAG VI/B, transferred to Colditz Castle. Lost both legs before the war in a flying accident but rejoined the RAF as a pilot in 1939. Famous for both his bravery and indefatigable spirit, his colourful and inspirational life was chronicled in the 1950s' book and film *Reach for the Sky*.

REED. My father's favourite master at Wixenford preparatory school, circa 1918/21. In 1934 the school closed and in 1937 Ludgrove preparatory school took over its former buildings. On numerous occasions my father told me that there was never a time as a POW that was quite as bad as the first term at his preparatory school.

DENIS ATKINSON. POW in OFLAG VI/B. He was 'not obvious friend material'.

HECTOR CHRISTIE (POW in OFLAG VII B. At one time trainer to Lady Lindsay. He trained 1947 Gold Cup winner Fortina), TONY ROLT (POW in OFLAG VII B, Rifle Brigade. Moved to Colditz Castle, later awarded a bar to his MC for his numerous escapes. Described as a grandee of the British motor-racing community, he went on to win Le Mans in 1953. He was also a talented engineer and was a driving force behind developing the Ferguson four-wheel drive system. In the late 1930s, Tony acquired the famous pale blue-and-yellow ERA racing car, Remus, from Old Etonian Siamese princes Chula Chakrabongse and Bira Birabongse. In 1959 Remus was acquired for the princely sum of seven hundred pounds by Patrick Lindsay, the father of a good friend of mine. It was a regular and hugely successful competitor in historic motor races until the family sold it in 2001).

GERRY PILKINGTON, JOHN CRIPPS, TERENCE PRITTE. POWs in OFLAG VII/B.

ALBERT. POW in OFLAG VII/B and friend of Peggy's. Possibly his last name was Arkwright.

ZARA MAINWARING. Married Ronnie Strutt on 15 November 1940. They had one son, Richard, born 24 October 1941, and the couple divorced in 1949. Zara married the Queen Mother's trainer, Peter Cazalet, the same year.

BELLAMOUN, BELLACOSE. Thoroughbred racehorses.

TONY LAWRENCE. Good friend. He died of cancer when only twenty-six.

PETER DODD. POW in OFLAG VII/B. He died following a session of PT.

JOHN LOYD. Close friend. He died from TB after returning home from Africa.

LEE WINDSOR (POW in OFLAG VII/B. He was very sensitive about his loss of hair), MICKEY SMILEY (POW in OLFLAG VII/B, Rifle Brigade. He was an old friend from Eton and RMC Sandhurst, previously MFH in Sussex, 'married one of the numerous Pearson girls [Lavinia]', 'hates losing at piquet'), PARKY GOUCOS (POW in OFLAG VII/B. He was rather obsessed by religious matters, COE in particular).

JOCELYN ABEL-SMITH. POW in OFLAG VII/B. His offspring is at Ludgrove preparatory school with Peggy's son/s.

MR DE Q. Presumably a big shot in the world of agriculture.

JACK POOLE (POW in OFLAG VII/B. He was an old friend and also a friend of the curious Mr de Q), JACK LESLIE (POW in OFLAG VII/B, of the Irish Guards. He was a delightful dreamer 'never quite on this Earth', whose father Sir Shane Leslie was an Irish diplomat, author and first cousin of Winston Churchill. Jack's sister, Anita, claimed, 'In my parents' view, schools performed the same functions that kennels did for dogs. They were places where pets could be conveniently deposited while their owners travelled.').

OLD LADY TREDEGAR (née Carnegie), Unusual octogenarian who, every year, felt the urge to construct extremely realistic birds' nests and then secrete them in inconvenient places.

MICHAEL PRICE (POW in OFLAG VII/B, aka 'The Prawn', affable hypochondriac), FITZ FLETCHER (POW in OFLAG VII/B aka 'The Rook', delightful man, 'successful in love'. Fitz Fletcher was my godfather, and a very good one, too!).

HYPERION. British-bred, thoroughbred horse. Hyperion was owned by Edward Stanley, 17th Earl of Derby, and was trained by George Lambton. Dual classics winner, St Leger Stakes and Epsom Derby in 1933, and later champion sire.

BLUE PETER. Thoroughbred horse. Blue Peter was both bred and owned by Harry Primrose 8th Earl of Rosebury, and was trained by George Lambton. Winner of the 2000 Guineas in 1939 and Epsom Derby, his racing career was cut short due to the outbreak of war, when the St Leger Stakes was cancelled. Subsequently a leading broodmare sire.

Prison Camps

As a general rule of thumb OFLAGs (short for *Offizier-slager*) were prisoner of war (POW) camps intended for officers. Other ranks were sent to STALAGS (short for *Stammlager*). This is a brief guide to the camps to which my father was sent.

OFLAG IX A
Spangenburg Castle, May 1940 to March 1941 and
June 1941 to October 1941

Schloss Spangenburg has a long and varied history stretching back to medieval times. It was a Gothic-inspired fortified castle, later used as a fortress and a hunting lodge before becoming a World War II POW camp.

It was primarily intended for British officers but in reality housed a mixture of British army, naval and RAF officers and some French inmates. Prisoners were either held in the castle itself or, as was the case for my father in September 1940, moved to the lower prison camp in Spangenburg.

Adapting to life as a POW was particularly challenging for my father. Food was strictly rationed and he had only the clothes he stood up in. But needs must and he was even obliged to tear off his shirt-tail to use as a handkerchief. Fellow POW and lifelong friend John Surtees remembers arriving in the camp and being greeted by my father.

'He was dispensing a plate of lettuce sandwiches to members of our two-dozen party. It was my bad luck not to be awarded one – an oversight which Roger was not allowed to forget for the next fifty years. It was the last sight of lettuce I had until 1945. We had been travelling by barge and cattle truck for fourteen days and we were famished.'

John was wearing French khaki knee-breeches and a blue pullover and my father had mistaken him for a Frenchmen. This apparently disqualified John from having rations intended for British officers!

Schloss Spangenburg ceased to be used as a prison camp in March 1945 and shortly afterwards was completely destroyed by an American air raid. It was totally rebuilt, reflecting its history, and is now, somewhat ironically, a rather smart hotel/restaurant.

STALAG XX A
Thorn, March 1941 to June 1941

Located in Thorn, Poland, the main camp was made up of a complex of some fifteen separate forts that had been built at the end of the nineteenth century in order to defend the

Prussian border. At its peak the camp contained as many as twenty thousand prisoners housed in the various forts.

My father and other POWs were sent here as a punishment in a tit-for-tat exercise because the Germans were under the impression, wrongly, as it happened, that German POWs held in Canada were being housed in substandard conditions.

My father wrote to his first cousins Tom and John Blackwell, 'You'd laugh yourself sick if you saw my new home. Dartmoor simply isn't in it. I've never lived below ground level before, but you soon get used to it. The weather is the worst part – bloody cold and still snowing.' Some of the rooms were permanently flooded with several inches of water.

On a more positive note, fellow POW and friend Francis Reed wrote, 'Thorn was a small camp and, although physically uncomfortable, seemed to have a happier atmosphere than many other camps – perhaps in part due to the excellent senior British officer, Brigadier Nigel Somerset.'

OFLAG VI B
Warburg, October 1941 to September 1942

Originally planned as an airfield, this purpose-built camp opened for POWs in September 1940. Described by fellow POW Francis Reed as a 'vast mud-heap of a camp', it consisted of numerous huts positioned on a high, exposed area surrounded by twelve-foot-high, double barbed-wire fences with a gap of some six feet between the fences, the void filled in with massive rolls of barbed wire. At approximately one-hundred-yard intervals there were watchtowers, equipped with hugely powerful search-lights and manned by heavily armed guards. In August 1942 there was a mass escape attempt known as the 'Warburg Wire Job'. Of the twenty-eight POWs who managed to break out, only three made it home. The following month all the British prisoners were transferred to other camps.

OFLAG VII B Block II
Eichstätt, September 1942 to April 1945

Situated next to Eichstätt, Bavaria, the camp was purpose-built in 1939 and consisted of a number of orderly rows of tall, brick buildings with tile roofs. It was originally home to some 1350 Polish prisoners, who vacated in May 1940, and later housed a variety of allied POWs, including Australians, Canadians, New Zealanders and South Africans. My father and his fellow prisoners were moved there in September 1942.

On 14 April 1945, as the US army approached, the officers were marched out of the camp towards Stalag VII A, Moosburg. Tragically, the column was attacked by American fighter planes who mistook the POWs for German soldiers. Fourteen British officers were killed and a further forty-six wounded.

My father's lifelong friend Desmond Parkinson wrote in his diary of that fateful journey, 'The most tragic, terrifying and emotional day of my life – anyway, as a prisoner . . . as the first plane came over, it opened fire and all others followed suit. Again and again the planes swept down and strafed us from practically road level. Mercifully, they must have used all their bombs on the lorries. By this time, Freddie, John, Morty and I were trying to make ourselves as small and inconspicuous as possible. We felt horribly exposed and very frightened. My first instincts were of self-preservation, but this soon gave way to complete fatalism, punctuated by prayers and thoughts of my family.'

'Morty' was my father, 'Freddie' was Freddie Burnaby-Atkins and 'John' was John Surtees. John and Freddie were very close friends of my father, along with Charlie 'Boots' Rome, Peter Black and Fitz Fletcher. All were on the same disastrous march on which, sadly, their mutual friend, Phil Denison, was killed.

Fifty Years On or Stray Bats From An Old Belfry

I left the Royal Military College (RMC) Sandhurst in December 1929. My career at that spartan establishment had not been unhappy, except during my first term, but it had been wholly lacking in distinction. In fact, I might never have succeeded in passing out at all but for 'special marks for effort' awarded me by my company commander, Major F. G. Chalmer DSO MC, of the Black Watch, who was alleged to favour Etonians and cadets who hunted. Not many of my contemporaries in No. 4 Company achieved fame subsequently, but Frank Furlong, killed flying in World War II, and Fulke Walwyn, for many years a highly successful trainer, both rode Reynoldsown to victory in the Grand National; Furlong in 1935, Walwyn the subsequent year. They both served in the 9th Lancers.

My place in the final passing-out list was a humble one and it was a relief to read in *The Times* newspaper

28

the following month that I had been gazetted to the Coldstream Guards. A friend of mine at the RMC had applied to join the Rifle Brigade but his record was indifferent and he found himself gazetted to the rather dim York and Lancaster Regiment, commonly known as the 'Pork and Doncaster'. In *The Times* this was abbreviated to the 'Y & L R'. My friend's reaction – hardly a wise one – was to write to the War Office in these terms: 'I asked to be gazetted to the Rifle Brigade: you have apparently apprenticed me to some obscure railway.'

My family had no connection with the Coldstream Guards. My grandfather and my father had both attained the modest rank of captain in the 60th Rifles (King's Royal Rifle Corps, KRRC), the former being wounded in the Indian mutiny, the latter in the great war in which he himself, a stockbroker, found himself a second lieutenant, aged thirty-five. His commanding officer, Lt. Col. Albert Paine, received my father kindly and invited him to come and see him at once if problems arose. Several times my father sought his advice, only to receive the answer, 'For God's sake, don't ask me. I'm the last person to know what's going on.' More than thirty years later, Colonel Paine was clerk of the course at Stratford-On-Avon racecourse. People used to watch the racing there from a flat roof above the weighing room. One afternoon this roof collapsed and a score of racegoers descended, feet first, into the weighing room below. The colonel, with typical sang-froid, was heard to observe, 'You know, I've been expecting this for years.'

My brother-in-law, Reggie Cockburn, also served in the 60th in the great war, being awarded the Military Cross

(MC). He and my father, between the wars, loved making battlefield tours in France. I can still recollect a rhyme my father enjoyed repeating about General Sir Cameron Shute, a Rifleman whose penchant was to make sudden swoops on units under his command, in order to inspect the latrines. In consequence, his nickname among the officers was 'Deus ex Latrina'. These inspections seldom afforded the general much satisfaction – rather the reverse, in fact, and he was liable to express himself strongly. Hence the following lines:

> The general inspecting the trenches
> was heard to exclaim with a shout
> 'I will not inspect a division
> that leaves its excreta about.'
> The division retained its composure
> and no one was heard to refute
> that the presence of shit in the trenches
> was preferred to the presence of Shute.

It had been planned for me to go into the 60th too but, unhappily, at the RMC I fell foul of an instructor from that regiment, Captain Le G. G. W. Horton, commonly known as 'Browndog' Horton. He later became an Eton master. A sincerely religious man, he took objection to what he considered to be my flippant attitude in the choir, a body I had joined solely to avoid the rigours and boredom of church parade (I was eventually turned out for making a nonsense of the 'Sevenfold Amen'). A conversation with Horton proved unfruitful for us both and he removed my name from the list of aspirants for the 60th, replacing it with that of an earnest Malburian, John Hunt, whose family was closely connected to the Indian army. Hunt eventually became senior under-officer of my company. I rather liked him, not least because, like me, he was atrociously bad at PT and loathed the sadistic instructors. In common with so many young men of lofty moral standards, he suffered badly from boils on the neck – the type known in the Coldstream as 'drill sergeants'.

I recollect that, as I was setting off one weekend, John Hunt called me over and said, 'Roger, if it comes to my ears that you have been consorting with any loose women, I shall never speak to you again.' As a matter of fact, I was going racing at Sandown so our friendship was in little peril of termination. He, in due course, joined the 60th, but I think that, despite many truly admirable qualities, he was something of a misfit there. In later life he led the first successful Everest expedition and received a peerage.

They were not a very exciting lot at Sandhurst, in my day, and few achieved military distinction. Ken Darling became a general. Though a contemporary of mine both at Eton and in No. 4 Company, I cannot recollect ever having exchanged a word with him before he became my brother-in-law. David Niven, an athletic character from Stowe, who enjoyed taking a rise out of the more pompous instructors, became a film star after a brief and turbulent career in the Highland Light Infantry. In his autobiography, he described the high standards demanded by the adjutant, Captain 'Boy' Browning of the Grenadiers. In fact, Browning had left Sandhurst before Niven ever went there, being succeeded by Captain E. J. Moore of the Royal Inniskilling Fusiliers.

Moore, a smart and agreeable character, was rather looked down on by Regimental Sergeant Major Pearson (late Coldstream) because he was not a Guardsman. Pearson sometimes used to say to the under-officers, 'Go on, salute the adjutant – it's good practice.' On church parade, Pearson was apt to give the order, 'March off the minor religions,' this designation covering Roman Catholics, Jews, Hindus and Mohammedans – in fact, all who did not belong to the Church of England (sometimes, in jocular mood, he would order, 'March off the mixed grill!').

I did not much care for Pearson and felt more at ease with Sgt. Ker of the Duke of Wellington's Regiment, who went in for poaching and betting. If one had had a rather sketchy shave, Ker used to remark, 'Fish for breakfast again. I can see the bones sticking out of your chin.'

Most of the equitation staff were easy to get on with, too, although the officer in charge, Major 'Bongo' Barrett, whose father had played cricked for Australia, was a gloomy martinet determined that no one should derive a hint of pleasure from riding instruction if he could possibly prevent it.

The language of the equitation sergeants tended to be colourful and I remember Sgt. Bird remarking, more in sorrow than in anger, 'If Jesus Christ on his way to Jerusalem rode 'is donkey as you're riding that here 'orse, then no wonder 'e got crucified.'

One of the horsier cadets was Hugh Jones, suspected of trying to 'fix' the RMC point-to-point. He went into the 10th Hussars, delighted his seniors by winning the Kadir Cup, the blue riband of pig-sticking, but rather spoilt the effect by doing a bolt soon afterwards with his squadron commander's wife. He later became an unsuccessful trainer.

As I said earlier, I had no connection at all with the Coldstream Guards, but my mother had an old boyfriend, a certain Colonel Wyld, who had served in the regiment and who subsequently held a position of some importance with Fortnum & Mason. He smoothed the path that led to my being accepted. I was not, in fact, particularly grateful at the time for his intervention as I frankly could not see myself settling down in what that genial Epsom trainer, the late Herbert Smith, described as 'one of them fucking fur 'at affairs'. However, at least I had fared better than some of my friends and acquaintances. Requested at the RMC to put down his first three choices in respect of regiments, Hugo Brassey wrote as follows:

1. The Royal Army Dental Corps (extraction section)
2. The Shitshire Light Infantry
3. The Blues

I think what he eventually received was a single ticket to Australia.

I joined the 3rd Bn. Coldstream Guards on the last Sunday in January at Chelsea barracks, about twenty minutes' walk from my parents' house in Cadogan Square. The 1st Bn. was also stationed in Chelsea. Arthur Pilkington, who had been in the same company at Sandhurst, was likewise joining the 3rd Bn. and we agreed to report to Chelsea together. We both knew very little about the Coldstream and were extremely nervous.

I did not own a car but Arthur had a blue, two-seater AC and, in this vehicle, we drove up to the guardroom. The sergeant, Gulliver by name, politely invited us to inform him of our names. Now, in moments of stress, Arthur was liable to stammer badly and, on this occasion, the word 'Pilkington' proved an insuperable barrier. After several rather painful attempts, Arthur lost his nerve, reversed his car at high speed back into the road and drove off. Ten minutes later we approached the guardroom again. This time, different tactics were employed. 'He's Mr Pilkington,' I said, 'and I'm Mr Mortimer.' Sgt. Gulliver directed us to the officers' mess and our careers with the Coldstream began.

Chelsea barracks in 1930 were grimy, uncomfortable and wholly unattractive – much inferior to Wellington barracks. On a Sunday evening in January it seemed dauntingly lonely and depressing. A search eventually revealed the portly form of the picquet officer, Angus McCorquodale (nicknamed 'Corkers'), tightly encased in a blue jumper and blue home-service trousers with a broad, red stripe – the common attire when not on parade for officers doing duty in London. A blue serge belt with a brass buckle was worn with the jumper (called, outside the Brigade of Guards, 'blue patrols'), never a leather Sam Browne belt. The closely fitting collar of the jumper had no washable – let alone detachable – lining, and it is grisly to picture how dirty it must have become, the jumper being sent to the cleaners perhaps once or twice a year. Footwear consisted of short, black, leather wellington boots.

Arthur and I unfortunately mistook Corkers for the mess sergeant, which was hardly calculated to ease the situation. Corkers was, in fact, as shy as Arthur and I were. He was reputed not to have spoken, except when directly addressed, during the first two years of his service. He was, in various respects, a unique character, a very delightful one when you got to know him, and an officer with an exceptionally high sense of duty. A good, all-round sportsman of robust health, he was alleged to have been unwell only once in his life, that memorable occasion eliciting a longish story which began, 'Well, once at Windsor I ate some fish.' He was killed when leading a company with great gallantry in France in 1940. He could never have been described as a ladies' man: the only woman he was known to speak to being another McCorquodale (not Barbara Cartland), a first cousin whom he eventually married. They were devoted to each other and, after Corkers' death, she seemed to lose interest in life and died not long afterwards.

The mess sergeant, Sgt. Mair, produced a servant for me, Gdsn. Wright, whom I met some years later as Corporal McDonald of the Scots Guards! The position of officer's servant – the terms 'batman' or 'orderly' were never used – was then a favoured one. During World War II, conscripts (and their girlfriends) tended to find the word 'servant' derogatory, and the duties involved beneath their dignity. The word 'servant', therefore, was deemed impermissible and the term 'orderly' substituted. Even so, it was seldom easy to find a man who actually volunteered for the job.

It was, however, a very different matter when I joined. A servant was exempt from almost all military duties and was rarely even called upon to wait in the mess, his life being almost wholly devoted to the welfare and comfort of the officer to whom he had been assigned. He usually wore plain clothes (dark suit, dark overcoat, bowler hat) and, if he had bought the clothes himself, he received an allowance of ten shillings a week from his master. If the latter had paid for them, he would receive five shillings a week. A weekly account for cleaning material and incidental expenses was also submitted.

It must be remembered that in those days most guardsmen received only ten shillings when they formed up for their weekly pay and that the purchasing power of a ten-shilling was not far short of a five-pound note today. Also, since he so rarely wore uniform, a servant made money on the clothing allowance provided by the army. His bearskin, greatcoat and cape, for example, were public clothing, which he received free, but tunics were his own property and he needed three of them: a 'best' for big occasions, a 'second-best', and one suitable for walking out in when he did so in uniform. A tunic then cost something over three pounds – a lot of money for a guardsman. It is hardly surprising that occasionally a guardsman who had been 'stopped' for a new tunic was tempted to earn a quick fiver by obliging some old gentleman with odd tastes in Hyde Park. Guardsmen with a reasonably good record could apply to their company commander for permission to wear plain clothes out of barracks. They had to produce a suit for the company commander's approval, and a hat – bowler or trilby – always had to be worn.

Most officers' servants learned to drive their master's car, which was an added attraction. They used to drive with their master's suitcase to St James's Palace, Buckingham

Palace or the Bank of England when the officer in question was on King's Guard or Bank picquet. On church parade, the servant paraded in plain clothes on the left of the line with his officer's cape over his arm. On the march up to the bank, the cape was carried by the drummer.

Many officers took their servant home on leave with them and, in those days, it was not unusual for a captain to have twenty weeks' leave a year, as well as most week-ends. In the case of a married officer, a servant was apt to become a member of the household and hardly ever saw barracks at all.

Generally speaking, the relationship between master and servant was good, and an officer who took pains to train his servant and to win his confidence was usually well rewarded. An occasional officer would be exacting and unreasonable, in consequence finding it difficult to retain a servant for any length of time. I am happy to say I am still in touch with my last servant, Birch, though we have not actually met for thirty-five years.

My first servant, Wright, went to the reserve after a few months and his place was taken by Gdsn. Birks, a tall Yorkshireman from Barnsley. Whenever I hear the place mentioned, I forget Arthur Scargill and Michael Parkinson and think of Birks. Everyone in the battalion knew and liked Charlie Birks, a great character with a dry and sometimes deflating sense of humour. In the war he became a sergeant and was decorated for gallantry. Sadly, he died of cancer not long after the war was over. Gdsn. Lee, my servant in the 1st Bn. in France, 1939–40, an extremely nice reservist, was killed together with my driver during the retreat to Dunkirk.

I remember well some of the outstanding servants in the 3rd Bn. over fifty years ago, particularly Croom and Skedgwell, who looked after Gerry Feilden and John Baillie respectively. They shared their masters' enthusiasm for the turf and I used to meet them racing at Newbury, until they both died a few years ago.

It must not be thought that officers' servants were unduly subservient: they knew too much about their masters to be wholly respectful. Not infrequently, noises and laughter emanating from the servants' 'kitchen' made it obvious that the voice and speech of certain officers were being imitated. 'Waitah, waitah, bring me a hot potatah on a cold plate!' I remember a slightly pompous officer shouting down the passage, 'Smith, I think I'll wear my blue suit this afternoon.' I heard Smith mutter as he passed me, ''E's only got one suit and that's blue.' A young servant, anxious to please but a trifle unpolished, said to his master, 'What 'at will you wear this afternoon, sir? Your flat cap or your cunt?'

Whether it was good for a young officer of twenty to be waited on hand and foot is a matter of opinion. Some soon became incapable of running a bath or changing for dinner without a servant hovering in attendance. As for packing a suitcase, that was quite out of the question. Matters were no better in the anteroom, and the manners of some officers tended to deteriorate. After reading a newspaper an officer would probably be too indolent to put it back on the table but would leave it, very likely inside out, on the floor. Empty glasses, too, would be left lying beside chairs on the floor. The rigmarole for making a telephone call was absurd. An officer would ring a bell to summon a waiter. The waiter, on arrival, would be told to ring up a certain number. He departed to the telephone box to do so and in due course arrived back to announce the call was 'through'. The officer then went to the telephone box himself and proceeded to carry out his business. It was not judged inconsiderate or bad manners to keep someone waiting on the other end of the line.

The waiters were certainly not overworked in the matter of fetching drinks, as the 3rd Bn. officers were remarkably abstemious and only one could be reckoned a hard drinker. The food was up to the standard of a good London club and was remarkably cheap. My monthly mess bill seldom exceeded ten pounds but, admittedly, I drank very little, and did not smoke at all.

One year at Aldershot I did notice that George Pereira, an easygoing and agreeable officer, was liable to have two large glasses of gin and French vermouth before lunch. At lunch, he had a pint of beer followed by two large glasses of vintage port. One evening he asked me if I could recommend him a good doctor. I expressed the hope that nothing serious was the matter, to which George replied, 'I don't think it's serious but I'm getting worried because I find it so desperately difficult to keep awake after lunch.'

George was a keen cricketer and a chain-smoker. Once we were both playing for Oliver Leese's team against the Broadmoor criminal lunatic asylum's eleven, composed partly of murderers, partly of patients. We had been warned not to smoke, as it was strictly forbidden at Broadmoor. This was too much for George who, while his side was batting, retired to the loo for a quick drag. Two wickets fell quickly and we had to shout to George to take his place at the crease. Fortunately, he was padded up, but forgot about the cigarette. Halfway to the wicket he remembered and nonchalantly chucked it away, whereupon about forty lunatics who were watching the match got up and fought like demons for the unexpended portion. There was really quite a nasty little scene.

Lunatics are apt to be nervous of dogs who, in an odd way, are suspicious of them. At one match, Malcolm Erskine unwisely took a rather weird lurcher of his, called Charles. In the pavilion, Charles discovered an inmate and advanced on him, growling ferociously. The poor chap then had hysterics and bit his own hands through to the bone.

The patients watched the cricket keenly, recording the scores in little books. Rather oddly, they always favoured the visiting side and, when you got the chaplain out, they all used to stand up and cheer. I met one or two well-known murderers there, including Ronald True, a suave and cheerful individual who had strangled a tart in the Fulham Road. True always gave visitors a hearty welcome. There was also Col. Rutherford, who had shot his second-in-command whom he suspected, quite wrongly, of doing Mrs Rutherford, a severe lady with distinctly limited sex appeal. The colonel used to ask abstruse military questions about trends in mechanisation, questions that we were usually quite unable to answer.

Years later, after I had married, I lived at Yateley, a few miles from Broadmoor. One day, returning from Kempton, I found police patrols on every road and soon realised that there had been an escape from Broadmoor. In fact, two men had got away. 'One of them,' according to a police sergeant, 'was a very harmless individual who thought he was John the Baptist, while the other was a former schoolmaster with very disgusting habits.' Poor John the Baptist was speedily recaptured but the school-master got clean away and, in fact, held down the job of games master at a leading preparatory school on the south coast until his disgusting habits landed him in the soup again.

My eighteen months at Sandhurst had been spent mostly in drilling on the square and in cleaning my kit, no attempt being made to prepare me for my work as an officer. I did not have to buff up my kit at Chelsea but it was disconcerting to find I was back on the square again, drilling in the ranks. Routine, before I was passed off the square by the adjutant some three months later, was roughly as follows.

At 8 a.m. I attended adjutant's orders and learned a little of the way the battalion was run. This was followed by breakfast. No hot food was laid out in the dining room and one seized a morning paper, rang the bell and ordered from a waiter just what one happened to fancy.

At 9 a.m. I attended adjutant's parade. It always seemed to take very long time before the NCOs had been inspected, the roll called and the parade properly formed up. Eventually, I joined the corporals and guardsmen and was put through my paces for an hour. I then rushed off to company orders and then came a period of weapon train-ing, conducted by Sgt. Tombs, a portly, kindly man with a heavy moustache who habitually referred to everyone as 'this individual' and who had no gift for imparting a glimmer of interest into a very dull subject. Sometimes weapon training was taken by Sgt. Flint, who looked like a budgerigar, was army billiards champion, a confirmed wife-beater, and who eventually committed suicide.

At midday I had to go to commanding officer's orders, where my prime concern was to make myself as inconspicuous as possible. I recollect being appalled by the fearful noise made when the accused, escort and witnesses were marched in, marked time, halted and then turned to the right to face the commanding officer. All that stamping on a wooden floor, by big men wearing nailed boots, was very hard on the eardrums and, in my view, seemed totally unnecessary.

As far as the officers were concerned, the day's work was usually over at the conclusion of commanding officer's orders, but most officers did not leave barracks before tucking into a three- or four-course lunch. The commanding officer rarely wore uniform to take orders, being attired as if for a stroll down St James's Street. If, by chance, he came into barracks in uniform, it was an ominous sign that something – probably unpleasant – was afoot.

I remember soon after joining, a very tall, very shrewd officer called John Lascelles, who had obtained some fame – some might say notoriety – as a card player, said to me, "You will hear a lot of balls about the "Coldstream spirit". Shall I tell you what it is? It is the spirit that induces me to come into barracks at 10.30 in plain clothes to do my work, and very little work at that.'

Not long before World War II, John was given command of a battalion. I remember on some tiresome brigade exercise, he had to summon his 0 group at 3 a.m. He hardly looked at his best before dawn and one or two attached officers were a little surprised when he observed, 'You might not think it to look at me now, boys, but I was had a good deal at Eton in my day.' Sadly, John contracted a fearful kidney disease and died early in 1940.

My own day did not end at midday and, at two o'clock, I was back on the square for more drill in the ranks, this being varied from time to time with sword drill and colour drill. From 3.30 p.m. onwards, the day was my own. I was not yet the owner of a car, so frequently strolled up to the Guards Club for tea, or else to the Bachelors' Club, then on the corner of Piccadilly and Hamilton Place, which I had joined when I was eighteen.

The Guards' Club, situated in Brook Street and boasting two squash courts, was a perfectly agreeable place, although it was the tiresome fashion of officers to run it down. Lunch, I think, cost three shillings and six pence; dinner five shillings, while a single room for the night was seven shillings and sixpence. There were two admirable waiters, Hewitt and Hawkins, the former rather fat, the latter thin and with a hacking cough. Both did their job well, though inclined to be 'bold' with members they disliked. Hewitt eventually got into trouble for watering Jimmy Hennessy's brandy and was sacked. Coldstream subalterns and ensigns formed to protest and one officer went rather far in suggesting that Hennessy was lucky in so far as it was only water in his drink and not strychnine. There was much ill-feeling for a time between the Coldstream and Grenadiers. We could not obtain a reprieve for Hewitt but organised a subscription for him. If I close my eyes and cast my mind back fifty years, I can still hear Hewitt giving a dreadful cough and then shouting down the lift shaft, 'Indian tea and a slice of guards cake for Col. Luxmoore-Ball.'

The secretary of the Guards' Club was called Fletcher and the club was known to Coldstream officers as 'Fletcher's'. Old Fletcher used to get rather sloshed and talk to himself. I remember him slumping into an armchair one evening and announcing, 'God, Fletcher, you are drunk tonight!' On another occasion, lunching by himself, he suddenly put his knife and fork down and exclaimed, 'Don't worry, Fletcher, old boy, she's only a bloody little bitch.'

The following year I joined Pratts, being elected a couple of months after putting my name down. Nowadays, I believe it is several years before a candidate can hope to be elected. Pratts was then owned (I think) and run by Willie Walsh, later Lord Ormthwaite, a former Rifleman whose military career was rumoured to have been blighted when he was sick during dinner at Windsor Castle. Willie was a kind old boy, a fearful snob who rather enjoyed having his leg pulled. During his heyday, Pratts was was often referred to 'Walsh's'. As an impecunious ensign (my father added three hundred pounds a year to my army pay of about £120), I could afford to belong to three London clubs, the total amount being paid by me in annual subscriptions being about a fifth of what I now cough up for the Turf Club, where a double room for a single night costs £37!

My prowess on the square was guided by Regimental Sergeant Major 'Tipper' Davis and by drill Sgts. Printer and Vickers. All had been decorated for gallantry in the great war, all had moustaches.

Davis, later a very popular quartermaster of the 3rd battalion, used rhyming slang a lot though not, needless to say, when addressing the commanding officer. When drilling the battalion he sometimes played for laughs. 'Your drill's 'orrible,' he would shout. 'It's lifeless – just like yer oojipoo when yer pulls it out!' This was permissible at Chelsea, where the square was hidden from the public, but it was thought to be going a bit too far at Wellington barracks, where there were always a lot of spectators gawping through the railings. In those days, there was a curious female character called 'Bank Picquet Kate', who always marched with the Bank picquet from Wellington right up to the Bank of England. There was also a female flasher whose custom it was to divert men on parade by opening her coat to show she had nothing on underneath.

Drill Sgt. Printer later transferred to the Green Howards as Regimental Sergeant Major. This excellent regiment differed in certain respects from the Coldstream and attached less importance to drill. Always prone to exaggeration, Printer said that on his first battalion parade with his new outfit he felt like 'Gandhi at the head of a mob'.

When the Buffs (Royal East Kent Regiment) included in their rugby football XV a Siamese officer attached, Printer objected to the presence of what he termed 'a horrible Apache', 'Apache' being pronounced with a long 'A'.

Once Printer was searching for some minor miscreant and, kicking on a locked latrine door, bellowed, 'Who's there?' The surprising answer was, 'Jesus Christ, drill sergeant.' This witticism did not pay off as the next day the perpetrator was marched before the commanding officer, the charge being, 'Attempting to deceive the drill sergeant in waiting, i.e. stating he was Jesus Christ when knowing full well that such was not the case.' On leaving the army, Printer joined a leading London bank and could often be seen, a handsome and dignified figure, at functions of the London branch of the Coldstreamers Association.

1940

1940

1st Reinforcements
2nd Coldstream Guards
1st Infantry Base Depot
BEF

22 February

Dear Peggy,

I was delighted to get your letter today. It was great fun to read and will keep me pleasantly busy afterwards, firstly trying like hell to read the bit you crossed out and then racking my mind to put names to the hero and heroine of your story.

I'm still busy reading the books you sent me. I love Saki's stories, particularly those when children score heavily over their obnoxious relatives: how I wish I had had sufficient gumption and intelligence to do the same! *The Ascent Of F6* is as good to read as it was to see and hear on the stage, and the other one, though by no means on the same level, has some very lovely verses in it. Anyway, it was an awfully nice present, especially to a comparative stranger!

I must apologise for any letter I write being entirely egotistical, but in addition to being alarmingly self-centred, I don't see many people here. Do you know John Hislop, who used to work with Victor Gilpin? I've just had a letter from him in which he states that he'd just moved to a new billet which was very comfortable but with a rather sickly smell which at first he couldn't locate. However, after a day he ran it to ground and discovered the owner of the property in a state of semi-embalmment, 'laid out' in the bath. He'd already been dead a week, but couldn't be buried as the ground was so frozen that they couldn't turn a sod of turf: he remained in status quo for about four more days 'til the thaw set in, the cold having luckily kept him fairly fresh in the interim.

I hope you haven't got influenza as you thought and that your husband is better again. I've been playing football this afternoon and was severely kicked in the Adam's apple, which served me right for being such a bloody fool in playing at all. I certainly shan't play again: when you reach the age of thirty you begin to realise you are but mortal.

At the risk of boring you into a complete coma, I'll tell you of our night out here. I wrote to Ronald about it, but I hope he wasn't ass enough to show you the 'unabridged' version.

Four of us who live fairly close together (Arthur Fortescue, Ronald Speed, Tommy Gore-Browne and myself) decided to indulge in the invented luxury of a small party. We began with an admirable dinner with a good deal of excellent champagne and then decided to visit the local 'Bag of Nails'. It didn't require a very long inspection to discover that this was probably one of the dimmest and most sordid places on the face of the globe. An elderly gramophone (probably Thos. Edison's original model) gushed up some equally ancient music, a handful of exceptionally democratic officers were behaving like the less likeable sort of undergraduate, while the picture was completed by a troupe of elderly trollops who had probably seen service during the siege of Paris. However, we found ourselves in a state of mild hilarity by drinking a lot of very sweet champagne and I'm ashamed to say that eventually I sneaked upstairs with the lady who combined the most charm in proportion to lack of BO, while Arthur, a nice intellectual Wykehamist, sidled off with a dumpy little number who I expect was taller in the prone position than she was standing up. I will draw a curtain over what followed and will merely add that I soon returned feeling that in addition to a regrettable lapse from self-respect and good taste, I had wasted fifteen shillings.

The party continued in unabated good humour but at midnight the grins were wiped off our faces with remarkable suddenness when we found that it had snowed like hell, the roads were blocked and we were marooned in these regrettable surroundings.

A brief period of haggling with a hideous 'madame' followed, but at length we were given two rooms. The one that Arthur and I took was a little peculiar, as the walls and ceiling were made of looking-glass, I suppose in order that the more exotic clients, in addition to satisfying their urges, could watch themselves doing it in triplicate. Undeterred, we climbed into the master bed without even removing our boots, but unfortunately we couldn't find the electric light switch. The result was that wherever we might choose to look, we were confronted with our own flushed features, reflected hideously in tarnished mirrors and surrounded by the revolting sanitary equipment of the room's rightful owner. It was looking up at the ceiling that really did us in: there the mirrors were distorted and we saw ourselves stretched out side by side in quadruplicate, surrounded on every side by innumerable 'bidets' – just like some monstrous surrealist picture.

Almost as soon as we had dropped off into a sort of uneasy coma that could hardly be dignified by the name of sleep, the door was flung open and in came the room's owner with a particularly odious officer in the Suffolk Regiment who I last remember behaving with intolerable jollity on board a troop ship. Optimistically, I asked if they'd awfully mind indulging their beastly libidos on the floor – they did mind. So we moved off to less luxurious but more normal quarters, where we soon fell into a deep sleep.

Luckily, it thawed next day and we made good our escape. What my companions did in the meantime, I cannot in all decency disclose but I think we're all slightly ashamed and don't refer to the evening much.

I'm keeping the list of books you sent 'til I am short and then I shall immediately try and impose on you again.

If Ronald is lugging round debutantes he's a bigger bloody fool than I ever took him for. They're practically all the most shocking bores and only enjoy doing the dullest possible things. I'd sooner have the toothache than take out the average debutante. Personally, I would back you to take on about six at a time, bound, handcuffed, and starting after any disadvantage they cared to name.

Best love,

Roger

PS: I'm not surprised you don't like Eugene O'Neill's plays. I think they might be better if acted by competent Americans instead of the very intense English persons who are under the delusion that they're taking part in a very great work of art. Personally my tastes are distinctly lowbrow; in fact it is difficult to tell where my hair stops and my eyebrows begin. I can never take the likes of James Joyce really seriously, any more than O'Neill's plays. I have little sense of humour, but a certain sense of the ludicrous which always makes it difficult to treat serious people with the respect they deserve. At any rate, I think O'Neill, to use a vulgar Canadian expression, 'shoots a phony line of heifer dust'.

Personally, I should go to *Desire Under the Elms* if Flanagan took the part of the old man, Groucho Marx as his son and Beatrice Lillie as the wife.

I've just read two quite enjoyable books, *Portrait of a Young Man* and David Cecil's *The Young Melbourne*.

1st Bn. Coldstream Guards
BEF

Spring 1940

Dear Peggy,

I'm so sorry to hear that you're a victim of that almost universal but not particularly distressing complaint, German measles. I hope you've recovered all right and managed to take a few pounds off by fasting in bed.

In reply to your question as to whether I'm a moron, the answer is yes, pretty nearly. Given reasonable food, plenty of books and a warm room, I'm quite contented. I have no desire whatsoever for human company, fresh air, and least of all, for any emotional outlet. I'm perfectly certain that if you can't live with someone you're very fond of, the next best thing is to live alone. I don't much like the human race (with a few exceptions) and the less I see of it the happier I am.

I enjoyed *Tight Little Island* a good deal: it's not often that you can read a book that is both witty and exciting. My only regret was that the smug young undergraduate didn't get eaten: how sadly typical of his age and class he is, a nasty mixture of sententiousness and facetiousness. I think the author tends to overestimate the effect of the change of life on the average woman's behaviour, but I'm afraid it's a question that I've never seriously pondered over. I should like to have your views about it: anyway, if women are to be segregated during the transitional phase, I think it would be just as well to reserve an island for those old gentlemen whose prostate gland troubles induce them into such indecorous lapses from good taste. I like the cannibal chief a lot, his views on Christianity being particularly sound.

Not much sign of spring here yet so you're luckily spared a page and a half à la Beverley Nichols. The French don't go in for flowers much, but we have a lot of violets in our garden here, and some snowdrops, while I have put in some polyanthus with varying success: however we've got about 5,000 frogs mating in the pond: they are quite shameless and rather noisy and have given the guardsmen a good deal of amusement.

I went away for three days to umpire some dreary manoeuvres 60 miles from here: it was beautifully warm and nice country so I'm afraid I avoided all military activity and wandered about by myself. I came across a British cemetery behind a farm: it was quite a small one, not more than 24 people being buried there, but it is most carefully looked after and, with its rose trees and smooth lawn it contrasts very strongly with the surrounding country and is somehow rather impressive. Most of the poor devils inside seemed to be wretched boys of under 20: it's only when you get to our age, that you can realise how very young one is at 18 or 19.

Yours,
Roger

1st Reinforcements
2nd Coldstream Guards
1st Infantry Base Depot
BEF

March 1940

Dear Peggy,

I had no idea that you were a painter: I hope you do portraits as I should very much like to see one of Ronald, looking rather sourly blank and scratching his nose, exhibited in some London gallery. I'm scarcely surprised to hear that he has discarded his debutantes: being fully conversant with his views on them and also with his limited supply of tolerance, I had an idea that it was no more than a passing fancy. I agree that Ronald is no deb's delight: he is far too nice a person to be that. I think he would rapidly bore them almost to extinction, not that that is a criticism, for everyone is a pretty good bore to at least 50 per cent of the people they know and it's probably better in that case to have your failures with the very young and stupid.

I was interested to hear your views about Greta Garbo: I've never fancied her myself as she's always given me the impression of being rather a solemn bore and I don't personally rate her sex appeal at all highly, but that is purely a case of personal preference, and for that class of thing give me Ginger Rogers or Deanna Durbin.

I've had to move house this week and I'm now resident at Chateau . . . , property of Comte de M. I could never have believed that such a house and such inhabitants could possibly exist except perhaps in some remote corner of southern Ireland: it's just like one of the really macabre chapters from one of Balzac's novels.

The chateau is about a hundred years old and I shouldn't think painter, carpenter, or even a charwoman has set foot in it since its completion. It comprises some twenty bedrooms, six reception rooms but no 'usual offices' except a communal earth closet and a cracked sink. The walls are discoloured and streaked with damp, the floors are stained and bare and every room is crammed with junk that can scarcely be dignified by the word 'furniture' – broken tables, chairs with missing legs, cupboards full of dreadful quasi-religious ornaments that you couldn't put on the 'white elephant' stall at a church bazaar. The pictures, ruined by years of damp, vary from horrifying close-ups of sacred hearts to English sporting prints: in my bedroom a set of dismal Cecil Aldins (everyone beautifully mounted, no wine and no one falling except a rather common person in a bowler hat) jostle up against a very lively and imaginative work portraying the day of atonement. The ceilings are almost non-existent, there is no electric light and a dreadful graveyard smell pervades the whole place. In the room where I work, a long chain descends from the ceiling, but instead of supporting some form of illumination, a dreadful stuffed sparrowhawk, with a label flapping around its leg, sways sadly from the end of it, rocking monotonously to and fro in one of the many draughts that come whistling from the broken windows.

The residents fit in nicely with the furniture: the

count, whose income is possibly £100 per year, is a tall, dirty man with a mop of hair like a station lavatory brush. His aristocratic origin prevents him from working so he passes the day in regretting the Bourbons and complaining about the English: as a matter of fact, the last regiment here did strain the Entente Cordiale a bit. They pulled down his newest barn for firewood, laid him out when he protested, stole his wife's ring and tried to rape his daughters behind a heap of manure. He is just a ridiculous figure, a lazy, decadent, old snob but somehow rather pathetic.

His wife is a cripple and does the work of about five English servants: she has a horrible maniac's laugh that terrifies me. There are two daughters, nice simple things who work like peasants but we are not allowed to mix with them. Their life must be dreary beyond words and I am terribly sorry for them. There is also a lunatic son who can't talk: he doesn't appear in the day much but one is apt to run into him a bit after dark.

Tonight, my servant Guardsman Lee is taking the count and the daughters out to a cinema for a treat: I think this is one of the kindest things I've ever heard of as it will cost him a good deal and he can scarcely hope to get anything out of it.

Yes, I should love to read *Penguin Island* as I've never read anything of his at all. I did try Proust once but although I struggled pluckily I gave up the unequal contest after a bit. I'm always amused by Compton Mackenzie, although I have no doubt that he is a very tiresome person indeed.

I must go off now and see a general. Many thanks for

your letters and your great kindness in offering to send me books.

Yours sincerely,
Roger Mortimer

PS: my French is very indifferent, but not as bad as Eric Wyatt's, who got himself into a predicament by thinking that '*sage femme*' meant fortune-teller.

I recommend a novel called *Capricornia* by Xavier Herbert.

Please give my love to Ronald.

1st Bn. Coldstream Guards

April

Dear Peggy,

Many thanks for another superlative letter – quite one of the best – and that dirty postcard which has been greatly admired by my colleagues (except for one who just couldn't see the joke). I have about three regular correspondents whose letters give me a lot of fun and which I really look forward to – (1) Yours, which are legible, well-written, amusing and touch on pleasantly varied subjects such as racing, current literature, sex problems of later life, horticulture and ordinary scandal; (2) Sam Holdsworth, just plain pornography, very bad spelling, but very vivid powers of describing certain subjects in detail; (3) a nice debutante (they exist occasionally) called Hester Loyd, a remarkably astute observer of the pitiful absurdities of human nature, armed with a pretty acid wit. Good general gossip with an occasional twinge of vulgarity. Unfortunately, series No. 2 has stopped owing to the author being switched to the Arctic Circle where his fingers are probably too cold to hold a pen and there is probably very little scope for the type of exploit that suits his particular style of literature.

Ronald wrote to me the other day and said, 'Peggy is behaving quite well,' which means absolutely nothing to me, but sounds as if you were mentally unstable and apt to give way to distressing outbreaks from time to time. He said also he'd been guarding a colonel who is awaiting trial for that particular brand of vice which is found among

Church of England parsons and schoolmasters. The colonel said he'd being doing it for twenty years and had no idea it wasn't allowed! (I always have thought that most colonels are really very simple people.)

I wish Ronald was out here as I've found a place where they give the most extraordinary 'exhibitions'. The proprietor of this place is a retired trollop called Madame Koko who built up a snug little business by catering for the carnal needs of German GHQ during the last war. She is really a most amusing person with a considerable repertoire of anecdotes (that makes her sound a cracking bore, which isn't the case at all) and I enjoy many quiet evenings talking to her in her private sanctum: it is rather fun, too, listening to her when she has to go into the bar to bargain with a client or deal with refractory drunken officers, whom she deals with, with masterly ease.

I think it was very mean of your husband and extremely stupid of you yourself not to ask at least one really plain girl to your anniversary party: it might have made all the difference to your pleasure.

As a matter of fact I think you're good-looking in an unusual way and what's more, I'll back you in ten years' time to be able to whack all the others who were at your party. I think you're a stayer as far as looks and figure are concerned.

It must have been exciting waiting for that man to come boldly forward and do the dramatic at Quaglino's. Scenes like that are great fun and if you're lucky enough to be present at one, you can dine out on the story for at least a fortnight. I'm afraid I'm never likely to figure as one of the central figures as I'm far too unambitious and unsuccessful to pinch anyone else's girl and I don't give a damn if anyone ever takes one off my hands.

I'll certainly try and get you *Lady Chatterley* before I come on leave. Personally, I didn't like it much. (Why is it that sexually unsuccessful men write the most erotic books, i.e. Lawrence, George Moore?)

I feel a little embarrassed at your reading my letters to Ronald, rather as if you'd caught me in the nude before we'd been introduced! God knows what sort of rot I wrote in them, but I don't think I even actually write in cold blood what you seemed to expect. Anyway, if he's going to do that sort of thing to me, I'll show you one or two of his when I'm on leave that will finally lift the scales from your eyes and show you the monstrous lecher with whom you are dealing.

I get very little time to read now as pressure of work has greatly increased. Have you ever read *The Martyr* by Liam O'Flaherty? It is amusing and exciting with a strong touch of horror. It's about an intellectual rebel in Ireland with a strange religious martyrdom complex. He gets captured by a rather likeable sadist who forces him to assist in his own crucifixion. It's very well written but I don't advise it if you know nothing at all about Ireland in 1920-21, as that makes the characters and setting hard to understand. I'm very interested in Irish history and problems and am always prepared to be a pretty savage bore about it when offered the slightest chance.

I should think that the three-year-olds are a very poor lot this year. I've seen Dyebel who is not a great looker but he has, as you say, a good head of the old-fashioned type and a great action. I suppose English breeders will eventually, through sheer lack of success, be forced to stop breeding solely for good sales and two-year-old winners. I have a lot of tiresome theories about this but don't worry, I'll let you off that.

I've just had a letter which contains the following interesting sentence: 'Did you hear the story of Mrs "Flash" Kellett's reason for wanting to go to Palestine? I expect you did, so I won't waste ink on it.' Of course I don't know: can you enlighten me?

I have opened my tennis season and am playing very well but rather unfairly.

With best love and a great big wet kiss anywhere you fancy,

Roger

1st Bn. Coldstream Guards
BEF

April

Dear Peggy,

Once again, many thanks for being so kind to me. I'll certainly write in due course and let you know how I liked the books, although I'm afraid I don't get nearly so much time for reading up here.

I came up here a fortnight ago at four hours' notice and had the usual military journey – delays, discomfort and mild chaos. I was in the train for over two days and spent one night in between at what was mistakenly called a rest camp. There I had a rather troubled night dossing on the floor of a bathroom with four other officers. My feet pillowed the venerable head of some aged major, while I was alternately gagged and asphyxiated by a couple of rather warm feet which I fancy emanated from an elderly ensign in the Pioneer Corps. Eventually I arrived at the Bar at 5pm, whacked, and with the worst cold I've ever had. I intended to go straight to bed but relentless authority decreed at 7pm I should be seated in a howling blizzard at the front of a lorry with no windscreen for a two-hour drive. On arrival at our destination feeling like a block of ice, Walls' best, I was invited to march home, which I did, getting there for breakfast. Strangely, this vigorous treatment cured my cold.

We work very hard indeed, digging from dawn till dusk and route marching occasionally as a relief, but it is not unenjoyable and even interesting in a way. We have a company mess in an extremely comfortable house with good WCs and baths. I sleep next door, at the mansion of a wealthy local industrialist who is the proud progenitor of seven children under the age of twelve. As a matter of fact, I'm very fond of children once they succeed in learning the elementary principle of self-control and I look forward to my half-hour with them every evening: it makes me feel pleasantly domesticated and helps me forget the war for a bit.

Have you read Graham Greene's new book, *The Power and the Glory*? I've always been a fan of his since I read *Brighton Rock*.

You must have had a worrying time with Philip in bed with pleurisy: I've always heard that it's infernally painful and takes a long time to get rid of.

I hear Ronald is back at work at last, which is all for the good: I do think he's a callous swine only to write to me once, but I'll take it out of him when I next see him: I'm even considering furnishing you with one or two interesting facts about his past so that you'll be able to counterattack strongly next time he turns sour on you. I consider that your idea of a love letter from Ronald is mere 'wishful thinking' in its most exaggerated form. I can conceive of no more unlikely event. Firstly, he's too reserved; secondly, he's got too sharp a sense of the absurd and, thirdly, he's far too illiterate.

I'm afraid this letter is more than usually dull and ill-written but I'm very tired and am discussing tiresome military details at the same time.

I hope I'll see you when I come on leave in about two weeks' time.

Yours sincerely,

Roger Mortimer

1st Bn. Coldstream Guards

24 April

Dear Peggy,

Thank you so much for another letter. I can only say that I enjoy them even more than the arrival of the Racing Calendar, which is saying a great deal!

I'm glad to say that the tension here has subsided, leaving me feeling rather old and tired and, what's more, rather a bloody fool for ever having taken it so seriously. But my elders and betters were so grim and gloomy that I found it difficult to avoid developing a similar outlook. Anyway, now we are back at normal, and peace reigns supreme again.

The spring, thank God, has made a belated appearance: our cherry trees and magnolias are really magnificent, whilst the younger officers are coming out in unseemly spots and can sometimes be surprised reading Swinburne and Keats during the lunch interval. Even the hideous country where we are stationed has become almost beautiful, changing its appearance in the twinkling of an eye like the transformation scene in the last act of a Drury Lane pantomime.

I must say it's pretty rich being criticised as a complete lowbrow by Ronald: no one could ever take him for a Fellow of All Souls anyway. I admit I come under suspicion when I say that I have greatly enjoyed his company and conversation for the past nine years. We share a liking for dirty talk (and sometimes for a dirty act as well) but luckily, I do have other tastes, which I wouldn't dream of discussing with him as I know exactly what his reactions would be.

I read *War And Peace* for the first time this January. I agree with you that it is one of the greatest works of fiction ever written. I enjoyed the war rather more than the peace, being both intrigued and horrified by the criminal inefficiency of the Russian general staff and excited by the very vivid descriptions of the battles themselves, together with the adventures and mental reactions of the persons engaged in them. Natasha must have been very charming, although she had the unfortunate Russian trait of bursting into floods of tears about ten times a day. I liked fat Peter who got tight so often and really enjoyed himself but I thought Bolkonsky was a bit of a prig; besides being a very gloomy and sombre individual.

I wish I could see the French film of *Rasputin*. I've always taken a morbid interest in him, I think because I imagine him to have been one of the most terrifying and horrible persons of the last fifty years. I think the most frightening thing about him was the way he ate poisoned food without showing the slightest ill-effects afterwards.

The first film I saw of *Rasputin* was at least twenty years ago. I was sent off with my governess to see a tiresome travel film about South Africa but, by a great stroke of luck, the foolish woman went to the wrong cinema and we saw a vivid rendering of *Rasputin The Rascal Monk*. I remember she was dreadfully shocked by something in the film but firmly refused to explain to me what it was. My mother was as mad as a wet hen when I told her how I'd spent the afternoon.

Best love,
Roger

I liked that last book you sent me about lesbians: it's really very funny but rather cruel. How frightened I should be of women like that: do you think Ronald would have got on well with Cleo?

1st Bn. Coldstream Guards
BEF

13 May

Dear Peggy,

Just a hurried reply to your letter, quite the most amusing and interesting you have written to me: I'm keeping it to re-read in the rather frequent spasms of gloom that encompass me here from time to time.

We're in a state of advanced military activity here at present and everyone is terribly tense. I can't quite analyse my own reactions to the situation (which spares you a pageful of moralising bunk, mostly untrue) but I feel as if I was going to ride a rather chancy jumper in a race tomorrow and I'm not quite sure whether I want a hard frost to postpone it or not. Anyway, it's all rather exciting and I was only mildly upset when I found our parson ordering two hundred wooden crosses and a packet of labels for attaching to the kits of deceased officers!

I'm not sorry you thought my remark re: Beverly Nichols was a backhander at your most readable horticultural reminiscences; I felt I had to make some retaliation, however mild, for your suggestion that I was a moron, which unfortunately is probably nearer the truth than you imagined. Incidentally, I rather exaggerated in my statements about my dislike of the human race: but I'd been sitting for a month with an officer who's just as a guards officer would be portrayed in a play produced by the *Daily Worker*: in fact even the most ardent leftist would probably describe the part as rather overdrawn. I find this sort of person ignorant, prejudiced and insensitive and very trying to live with at close quarters, especially when he's considerably senior to myself and is apt to resent counter-criticism.

I was rather surprised at your view that even your best friends are bound to cast you sooner or later. I should hate to convince myself that that was true (as a matter of fact, I'm not sure whether you meant that and at any rate I'm mixing up love and friendship which are two different things). I agree that emotional and passionate relationships usually end in disillusionment as they are nearly always unequal in intensity of feeling and probably selfish on one side or the other: but I have one or two friendships which are based on rather less precarious stuff than passion (e.g. a few mutual dislikes or interest in racing!) and to which I owe the greater part of my happiness during the last ten years.

I'm so glad you like the Siegfried Sassoon poems: they are the bitterest things I've ever read. Some of his satire is so brilliant but as English people loathe satire, they're not very widely read. I'm not competent to say whether they're 'good' or not, but I like them myself *and* thoroughly agree with their sentiments. They are so very much better than the anaemic stuff on the same lines served up by young pacifists, because he was a gallant and efficient soldier himself and knew just how bloody war is: I know nothing about war at all, but I agree with you in loathing all that bogus heroic stuff which is so eagerly lapped up by a large proportion of that unlovely object – the general public.

How sadly true are your remarks upon trusting oneself: I only wish I could rely on myself in moments of difficulty but, alas, I fully realised I'm a very weak character and feel very lost if I haven't got someone with me whom I can really trust and upon whom I can throw most of the responsibility.

Give my love to Ronald,

Love from

Roger

A Letter Written In 1978 To Sir Peter Thorne, General 'Bulgy' Thorne's Son.

An amusing account of my father being captured in May 1940 and subsequent events.

Budds Farm
Burghclere
Newbury

21 March 1978

Dear Peter

<u>RE: Reichenau</u>

I have never written an account of what happened. It took place nearly thirty-eight years ago: I am now heading rapidly for seventy and my memory is probably more fallible than I myself choose to think it is. I cannot begin to remember the dates and the names of places in respect of this particular occurrence.

I was captured on the Dyle Canal, the Belgians on our left having departed during the night without giving any warning of their intention. A fairly unpleasant German officer told me I was to be shot immediately because the 'dirty British had begun using poison gas'. That little difficult blew over and I was given a room in a Belgian hospital for treatment for my left hand.

About two days later I was removed – I had no belongings at all – by two German officers who drove me off in a somewhat inferior car. True to form as regards most officers, they were unable to read a map and got hopelessly lost. I could understand a little German (having been taught some at Eton by 'Satan' Ford) and at one point the situation was so desperate that they were considering asking me to help them out.

We drove all through the night and the next morning ended up at a chateau with a lake in front of it. I was put in the charge of an agreeable officer who, as we sat in the garden, told me he always bought his clothes at Austin Reeds. I think he supposed that information would show him in a favourable light.

Eventually, I was told I was to be interviewed by Reichenau. I was in a fairly ropey condition and perhaps someone informed him of this, as I was taken to his bedroom where he sent his servant with washing and shaving things and a comb and, soon afterwards, his doctor arrived and applied a dressing. I was then led to Reichenau, whom I remember, in fact, less well than an urbane staff officer who looked like the film actor Edward Everett Horton, who was in most of the Fred Astaire–Ginger Rogers films.

Everyone was all smiles (except me) and I certainly remember being asked 'How is Bulgy Thorne? I have not seen him since Ascot.' The brief interview, which included no questioning on military matters, except the effectiveness of dive-bombing, concluded with Reichenau's advice to amuse myself in captivity by endeavouring to escape. Unfortunately, the officers in charge of prison camps took a less light-hearted view of that particular activity and only became more disagreeable if told I was only following a German field marshal's advice.

I had a quick look into Reichenau's suitcase, which was lying, packed, on his bed, and was slightly surprised to find it crammed with bottles of hair lotion, after-shave, etc., and very expensive, monogrammed shirts, pyjamas and underclothes, which looked as if they might have been purchased in the Burlington Arcade. On leaving the chateau, my standard of living and treatment suffered a painfully sharp descent.

In 1945, old von Rundstedt was in captivity in Kensington Palace Gardens, and the Westminster garrison, of which I was then second in command, supplied the guard. I rather liked the old boy, who was a striking contrast to most of the SS thugs and Gestapo murderers held there for questioning. I took him a drink one evening and we had quite a long military gossip. He told me that Reichenau had blood pressure and was inclined to drink too much. He was warned to keep off the brandy during long flights but failed to follow that advice and had a stroke.

I'm sorry I can't be more helpful but it is all such a long time ago and it is not a phase of my life that I often to care to look back upon.

Yours sincerely

Roger Mortimer

On active service

MORTIMER – in May 1940, killed in action, Roger Francis Mortimer, Captain, Coldstream Guards, only son of Haliburton and Dorothy Mortimer of 28 Cadogan Square, SW1, aged thirty.

MORTIMER, Captain Roger Francis, Coldstream Guards, previously reported killed in action, now reported to be a prisoner of war.

First letter as POW from OFLAG IX A

1940

OFLAG IX A

10 June

My dear Peggy,

I'm afraid this won't be a very amusing letter as discretion has to be given preference to attempted humour. The first nine days were the worst when I never saw another Englishman, had nothing to read and made constant train journeys in a very dusty and dishevelled condition and was the blushing recipient of considerable attention. It was a bore having only one hand in use when I was so entirely self-dependent but this is getting better now and has been well looked after. Most people have treated me quite well and the front-line officers and soldiers were very helpful and sympathetic. I'm living at present in a medieval castle, complete with wild boars in the moat in pleasant surroundings. I suppose after thirty years of ease, a little discomfort is good for one, but I hate never having a bath and having only one suit of clothes. The food is sufficient for this sort of life but I feel permanently hungry although very well so probably the diet is beneficial. There are books here but most of them are very inferior thrillers. I sleep in a room with ten double bunkbeds, in company with eighteen naval officers who have been very kind and who help one to preserve a reasonably sane outlook. We have a tiny garden where we toil in the morning, read or sleep in the afternoon, bridge after supper. Of course we get no English news and it's a great worry not knowing what is happening to one's friends. One is so completely cut off from all one's former surroundings that it's like starting a new life. Still, it might be far worse and I only hope the war won't last for years. Do write if you can.

Yours sincerely,

Roger

OFLAG IX A

(August/September 1940)

My dear Peggy,

I can never repay your kindness in writing to me so often. It must be so boring for you never getting any reply: letters make the hell of a lot of difference here, and a blank post is an awful disappointment. I hoped Ronald would write, but I haven't heard from him yet. Letters are coming through slowly but surely, and I've had about forty, the latest dated 24 July. I'm afraid the books you so kindly sent me haven't turned up yet. I'm getting pretty used to a convict's life and it could be a lot worse. The Germans leave us to run the inside of the camp as far as possible while they make sure we remain inside! It's a small camp with very few regular officers in it, only eight or so, of whom I know one. However, I'm in a room with nine very reasonable people so I'm not having my nervous system irretrievably irritated. Good manners are far more important in a prison camp than they are in ordinary life, and this type of existence is apt, after a bit, to bring out the worst in everyone. I hope you haven't wormed out of the bag yet as you've done Ronald a bit of good: write and tell me everything you can and don't fear the censor too much: I like to hear about persons, you or anyone else. Could you please send me if possible a couple of cheap novels by an acid female called M. S. Farrell and one called *The Mask of Dimitrios* and anything by the same man. The end of the war and release seems as remote as the moon. This strange life amid strange people makes me feel that I was killed in May.

Love from Roger

OFLAG IX A

13 November

Dear Peggy,

It's awfully nice of you to write every week and I've had twelve letters from you, the last dated 9 September. Many thanks, too, for *Pasquier* and *Hornblower* who arrived this morning. I'm not surprised you're out of the sack at last. I know R.'s form pretty well and it seldom varies. I shouldn't be surprised if he didn't rather dislike you now. He is very loyal and generous to his own sex, but his views on his friends of the other sex are subject to sudden and drastic changes. I never read your letters out to my friends here, but I did read that bit about 'prisoners developing rather odd habits'. We laughed over that. I hope you will take my word for it that in spite of the complete absence of female company, we show no definite signs of seeking irregular compensation! The small play I wrote was quite successful, especially a coarse scene in a headmaster's study. I'm now dramatising *Decline And Fall* by Waugh, my favourite novel. I've just finished a delightful book, *Gentle Savage*, by Richard Wyndham. I'm sure you'd like it. Our room still remains on excellent terms with one another: the conversation is pretty smutty but is has one great compensation: smut seldom leads to arguments and quarrels. I'm afraid I've become a ghastly prig and have a cold shower every day, do PT after breakfast and teach German after lunch. What with managing the library, art classes, etc. the time goes fast.

Best love,
Roger

PS: Your letters are *very* interesting, don't be so modest about them.

OFLAG IX A

22 December

Postcard

My dear Peggy,

I've loved your letters (thirteen of them) and I liked de Maupassant far better than any other book I've read in prison, with the Chinese book a good second. I'm looking forward to Yeats' poems. 'The Irish Airman Foresees his Death' is one of my favourites, together with 'Easter 1916', 'On A Political Prisoner' (Eva Gore-Booth) and the one that starts off, 'When you are old and grey and full of sleep'. Could you tell me if John Scott and Jack Price (9th) are both alive? Congratulations on what you've done for Ronald. I always said you'd brought him on two stone. I hope you'll do the same for me when I come out.

Love,
Roger

1941

1941

OFLAG IX A

4 January

Could you please forward this to Mrs Dunne, Chadshunt, Kineton, Warwick?

My dear Peggy,

Your letters come through splendidly. I've now had fifteen out of eighteen written up to 12 October. I was full of sympathy for you when you seemed so unhappy and I only hope your troubles and sorrows have passed. I am very well but going slightly mad, long periods of intense gloom being varied with short spells of senseless hilarity. Luckily, I find that prison seems to banish one's sexual desires so I don't suffer very badly in that respect. I had a slight accident the other day and hurt my leg and the doctor thinks I may go a bit short for life as a result. I've been as lame as a tree ever since and get no better. Your books have been a godsend and I think life will be easier to bear after reading the *Importance Of Living*. I hear that Jack Dennis has succeeded in having a 'romance' with a girl that many tried but found very cold and unreceptive – a good effort on his part. I'm learning veterinary work under an RAVC [Royal Army Veterinary Corps] colonel, which might be useful. I also do barber's work, sewing, darning and have even scraped someone's teeth, as well as some very unpleasant nursing work on New Year's Eve! I hope Ronald's marriage will succeed, but neither of them come from staying stock. Her mother's an awful old bitch. I'm very fond of R., but I'm a little sorry for the girl.

Love,
Roger

OFLAG IX A

4 February
To: Mrs Dunne, c/o Mrs Rankin

Dear Mrs Rankin,
I should be so grateful if you could forward this to Mrs Dunne, Chadshunt, Kineton, Warwickshire.

My dear Peggy,
Your letters and books do much to alleviate my rather dull and colourless life in prison. I've just finished *Hornblower*, which I liked far more than I expected and is a first-rate story, and the *The Priory*, which made me determined to marry someone capable and domineering after the war, like Nurse Pye. I read Yeats for half an hour every evening and am now beginning to appreciate some of the poems which seemed too obscure for me previously. I must say that you have a quite remarkable instinct for the sort of books that give me the greatest pleasure. I'm getting very fond of John Donne, too. I wish Ronald would summon the energy to write to me, otherwise we shall lose all contact and be complete strangers if I ever get out of here. If you have a small photograph of yourself, do please send me one and I shall be very interested to see your children too. How remote everything seems here. I hear of friends who have been killed and somehow it's awfully hard to realise that I shall never see them again: it's not a question of becoming callous, it's the result of everything here being so different and cut off from anything and everyone in one's past life. News from outside just seems

utterly unreal. Jim W. Lewis is an old friend of mine and I'm very fond of him. I heard he had put up a very good turn. Do you know anyone who could possibly send some food from America, as that country is easily our best source?

Best love,
from Roger

Moved to Stalag XX A
in March 1941

STALAG XX A

23 April, Good Friday
Postcard to: Mrs P. Dunne

Delighted to get some December letters from you after a two-month gap. I'm now in a different camp, where the accommodation is a little old-fashioned, but life is quite tolerable on the whole. Received with great pleasure parcel of books from you – two confiscated as unsuitable. Am reading and enjoying *Seven Men*. There's a young man here called Greenslade: I think his father is an art dealer in your county: he has just been doing a brief spell of 'solitary' for playing poker after lights out.

Love Roger

STALAG XX A

7 May

My dear Peggy

I had a January letter from you yesterday and a lot about the 'Cougar' nightclub was censored in England – at least twelve times. I can only conclude that our traditional English hypocrisy is averse to anything that might suggest we were not one hundred per cent moral. I also had a letter from Sophie Lyell in which some comments on a Scottish pantomime were similarly deleted. I would not frankly advise you to send your son to the school where Paul has been for the last year. The feeding is poor, from all accounts, with a strong tendency towards total vegetarianism. The masters vary: one is extraordinarily nice and helpful, while another resembles a burlesque of a schoolmaster by Nerdo at the Palladium. Another of the assistant masters is very bad-tempered and of course the pupils all nag him until he foams at the mouth and gets quite dangerously violent. The school buildings, too, are antiquated and hardly suitable for so large a school. I should recommend a more modern establishment, nearer home. Spring comes very late in this desolate country and we had snow yesterday. Are the frogs getting busy with their unattractive antics in your pond yet? I've been concentrating on my cooking lately and can now serve up a very sustaining meat pie, called 'Shepherds Bush', accompanied by a rich and glutinous sauce (*cream passionel*). I've got to like John Donne's poetry a lot, and read a little every night in bed. I find the local newspapers rather depressing to read: apparently we are relying entirely on two neutrals – God and the USA – to win the war for us. I heard today that my very young cousin, David Mitchell, has been killed. Our family war effort is now rather reduced – as out of five starters, two are dead, one in prison, one in hospital with boils on the bottom and only one in circulation.

Best love,

Roger

Back to Oflag IX A

OFLAG IX A

11 June

My dear Peggy,

Eight letters from you in one day last week, some December, others up till April. I'm so glad to have the photographs which I've framed and hung up by my bed. It is terribly kind of both you and Rose Fiske to take so much trouble on my behalf and I'm really more grateful than I can say. There's an American parcel waiting for me to open tomorrow and I am more excited than since Christmas Day when I was about six years old. I've left Poland and am back at IX A again. I'd worked very hard making a garden there, so I was terribly disappointed when I had to leave just when the lettuces, spinach and my herbaceous border were at last beginning to testify to my efforts and my obstinacy. The weather there was wonderful the last five weeks: straight from winter into really hot sun: and nothing to do most of the day except lie in the sun and forget the winter. Although the train journey back here was scarcely the height of comfort, it was wonderful to see the country again, particularly at this time of the year, with the trees at their best and acres of lilac. I shall miss not having the air force prisoners here. Most of them are from the Dominions and once you get to know them they are extraordinarily nice – kind, cheerful and most amusing. Marcus Marsh is amongst them. I'm pleased to hear that Ronald has rung the bell already. I somehow can't imagine him playing the part of fond parent. I have given up all hope of him ever writing to me. Jim Lewis is one of my greatest friends so give him my love. Tell Evelyn Waugh that Captain Grimes is a prisoner here. He is Grimes to the life, even down to Clutterbuck, and is never called anything else. I could write a whole letter about him.

Best love,
Roger

OFLAG IX A

12 July

My dear Peggy,

I've had shoals of most interesting and enjoyable letters from you lately, the latest being 18 May. The total is now forty-three which reflects considerable credit on your industry. I keep them all carefully tied together and I have no doubt extracts from them will feature largely in my biography some sixty years hence. Your photograph dropped out during censoring and was pinned on the public notice board to await claimant. I must say, it was most remarkably unflattering and it remained there forlornly for two days before I recognised it. I'll send you one of me, but I think I probably sent it months ago. I can't remember. I'm looking forward to the arrival of Mr Belloc's rhymes. Do you know his story 'The Mowing of a Field'? I have come to the conclusion that the best writers for prisoners are without doubt Evelyn Waugh and Siegfried Sassoon, with Aldous Huxley close up third. I can read them with pleasure when I'm too bored or too soured up to look at anything else. I am so sorry for you having to put up with an officious matron going through 'the change of life'. I could make two useful suggestions but I doubt if they would survive the censor. Perhaps it would be best to send her to Bedlam; that might keep her quiet for a bit. I laughed when you told me that my mother thought you were nourishing a secret passion for me: how disappointing for her if she only knew the circumstances of our friendship. Well, I must be off for my evening stewed prunes, so trying for the palate but most beneficial for the bowels. Your letters are never dull, and they really do alleviate my existence here. I think I've got a got a real life-sentence look about me now. I have just been told I look like an aged and despondent horse awaiting the arrival of the slaughterer.

    Love,
    Roger

OFLAG IX A

5 August

My dear Peggy,

I'm feeling in such an unusually good temper that I think I'd better write to you as you may get a change from my usual whines and complaints. I attribute my improvement to ten days of compulsory solitude; it was wonderful to be alone for the first time in over a year. I was allowed books and I just lay on my bed and read all day. I got a lot of fun from Samuel Butler and I liked *A High Wind in Jamaica*, although nothing will ever convince me that children allow the death of their brother (in most odd circumstances) to pass without comment. I also read *Elmer Gantry* and *Main Street* by Sinclair Lewis, the former quite excellent, three plays by Aristophanes, Plato's *Apologia*, and Trevelyan's *History Of England*. I'm afraid your book by Fisher is not allowed. Anyway, the change here has done me a lot of good, as my behaviour before was so objectionable that some people thought I was going through the change of life. I'm having lessons on the trumpet and I hope shortly to be able to give a fair rendering of Purcell's 'Trumpet Voluntary': can I come and play it as an anthem in your church after the war? At any rate, I may get the job blowing 'the off' at Kempton and Hurst. We have got some gramophones now but records are difficult to come by. However, we've got Beethoven's fourth and fifth symphonies and some quite good singing ones from *The Magic Flute* and *Figaro*. I think up until now I have missed music as much as anything else. Twelve of us have formed a syndicate and are buying a horse to be trained by Marcus Marsh who is also a captive. We are all anxious to hear if Jock Delves Broughton has 'swung' or not. Do tell me something about the trial if you can. I'll send you a revolting picture of myself, so nasty in fact that I feel I'm taking a needless risk in sending it. Please give my love to your children.

Best love and thanks.

Roger

OFLAG IX A

2 September

My dear Peggy,

Many thanks for your lovely letters as usual. I've kept them all most carefully and I think all but two have reached me. Will you please thank Rose Fiske for her very great kindness to me. I'm moving to a very nice room next week – only two others in it, both charming and easy-going people: the view from our window is really lovely. I'm looking forward to the change: after all, I've been living for a year on terms of honeymoon propinquity with nine very reasonable people, but we have all very sensibly decided to have a change before we start to loathe each other. When you begin to really detest someone whom you know is a really nice person, then obviously something has to be done. We're all going to feed together still and I'm certain our tempers will improve by seeing less of each other. Eight of us mess together and every parcel any of us receives is pooled except for sweets and chocolate. There is a weekly 'stooge' who lays the table, arranges the menu, looks after stores, makes puddings, etc. I loathe doing it, as indeed most of us do, but we are all pretty conscientious. The Red Cross are doing us very well now, and what with rations and other sources we live comfortably. We usually get up at 7.30, breakfast at 8.15, lunch at 12.15 and supper at 6 p.m. In addition, like domestic servants, we are very prone to cups of cocoa between meals. I think the two nicest and most useful people here are Nigel Courage, 15th/19th, who has lost a leg and Ossy Younger, Argyle and Sutherland, who is almost blind. I feel very ashamed of my frequent sulks when I think of their invariable politeness and good humour to bores and asses, especially as riding means so much to Nigel, while Ossy cannot read at all which makes prison twice as dreary.

Love,
Roger

OFLAG IX A

14 October

My dear Peggy,

I'm afraid you must think I'm not taking prison too well, judging from my usual dreary whining. Actually, it could easily be so very much worse. Of course the narrowness of it makes the indifferent people terribly mean and petty, but I have made some friends here whom I hope to retain as friends after the war. To my very great joy, some of the badly wounded ones are being repatriated soon. If you hear of them arriving in England, I only hope you will meet some of them and really understand how we live here. Nigel Courage, whom you may know, will be among them. There is a most delightful person, too, called Philip Moore: like a complete ass I forgot to give him your address so that he could give you some messages from me. He is the most unselfish person I have ever met, and the least complaining, although he lost his leg at the thigh and was over a year in hospital without a single letter from home, and only one other English person with him. He has promised to see Ronald for me so perhaps there is a chance you will meet him too. I hope you do, as besides being a very lovable person, he is intelligent and amusing and I'm certain you'd like him. I've been working hard lately at learning agriculture and have had a few really good laughs. It's a great relief to live in a small room with other people who are mad in much the same way as oneself. There are some very interesting psychological studies here: and certain aspects of prison life which you once mentioned are now rearing their heads in quite unexpected places. Many thanks for your letters. I like having your views on all sorts of abstract subjects.

Love,

Roger

What a very good photograph of you with the children.

Move to new camp

OFLAG VI B

17 October
To: Mrs P. Dunne

My address is OFLAG VI B. Battalion 2. I'm well.
    Love,
    Roger

OFLAG VI/B

4 November

My dear Peggy,

I've just got your very informative letter of 12 September and as is usual when I get a good letter, I feel impelled to make an immediate reply. I'm now settling in this new camp and feel in pretty good form in spite of a severe cold and a broken rib. I spent yesterday reading *For Whom the Bell Tolls*, the first Hemingway I've liked since *Death In The Afternoon*. I'm now re-reading *Life With Father*, which I love – did you send them to me? It sounds like your excellent taste if you did, very many thanks. It's been fun meeting so many new people here. Do you know Jack Faucus who rides for the Ranks? He seems an extremely nice person. Do you know Peter Dollar? I should like your opinion of him. I'm worried to hear you don't like the trumpet: personally, I pretty well loathe all brass wind, but I think the trumpet is less objectionable than most others. I'm certain it was a trumpet, and not a bugle, that played 'The Last Post' at Tiger Sudeley's funeral: a bugle is always perfectly bloody, but a cavalry trumpet, if well played, is superb. Do let me have any news of John Fox Strangways, if you get any. Ralph Cobbold told me he'd probably be permanently lame. I've succeeded at last in mastering the technique of detachment; in a room of sixteen, I can work or read in peace, regardless of what the other fifteen do: it is quite impossible to disturb me or annoy me. Since my summer solitude, my temper has been remarkably good, and I am even becoming quite charitable in my opinion of my fellow inmates.

Love,
Roger

OFLAG VI/B

3 December

My dear Peggy,
   Very many thanks for 2 October letters. I must admit that I've never paid less than a pound myself, so perhaps I've gone through life being hopelessly overcharged in the last fourteen years. The least I've ever heard is twice for a cake of soap. I do know, though, that a lot of them find the extra two-and-six here and there a great help to the old age pension. Do you know Rachel Willoughby? Years ago, twelve at least, I nurtured a hopeless and desperate love for her. Unfortunately, being morbidly shy, whenever I met her I could only sweat and make friendly noises – a fairly unattractive combination. However, I believe that even now if she switched those big eyes on to me, I should be reduced to the same awful condition in about five seconds. The entertainments here are pretty good, there being a fair number of prisoners. There is an excellent dance band led by a professional, and a promising symphony orchestra, forty-two players, conducted by Richard Wood who is a professional and performs at Glyndebourne etc., and Colonel Donald Fraser, who commanded the 16th Hussars. I was very worried to get a letter saying that R. was making rather an ass of himself and what a pity it was as his wife was so charming. As the writer was a woman who likes him but does not know him well, I have every hope that it is merely unkind gossip and quite untrue. In the unlikely event of the gossip having substantial foundation, I rather thought you might be the very person to give him a good

shaking. He is such an odd person – incredibly loyal and kind to friends of his own sex but rather the reverse with women. Many thanks for the books – there has been a big demand to borrow *Hocus Pocus* and *Brighton Rock*!

Well done Portobello.

Love,

Roger

OFLAG VI/B

3 December

Postcard

My dear Peggy,

My best wishes for the new year and I can never thank you enough for all you've done the past eighteen months for me. I'm afraid my letters are an epic in boredom but I'm sure you realise that it is not altogether my fault. Provided I'm not in prison for long, I think it may have done me a certain amount of good. Anyway, I feel in much better form than last year, have several friends who laugh at the same things, and am seldom unhappy except during prolonged constipation.

Roger

OFLAG VI/B

18 December
To: Mrs Dunne

I've had five letters from you today so I'm counter-attacking with two letters and a postcard. I wish you could come here for a weekend: we could have the most tremendous laugh and you'd meet some charming people and also some very odd ones indeed. Would you mind sharing a bed, not side by side with me, but on top, like bunks in a steamer? I've managed to get one or two books on house-building and am trying to improve my knowledge. I luckily have an extremely retentive memory as regards racing and at the end of a season I can guarantee to give the correct breeding of 95 per cent of the courses during the year. This may be due to an unsavoury habit of reading *Racing Up-To-Date* in the bath and *Horses In Training* on the WC. By the way, the best way for your children to learn geography is to have a good map hung up in the WC. What hell for you losing your nurse! I loved both of mine and wept horribly after they left, the last when I was fourteen although of course by then I was no longer under her sway. God, how I hated my governesses. I remember flooring one with a well-timed uppercut to the left breast and I've never regretted it for a second. The American parcels are excellent but I can't always tell from whom they come – and they have lovely tinned hams, milk, tea and tinned fruit and cocoa – all most welcome. I've arranged to send you an Easter present, which I hope you'll like. This place is in some ways like a girls' school – terrific 'pashes' and lots of smutty gossip. I'm playing Eton football on Sunday which is just bloody stupid at my age. We have a Christmas race meeting (an advanced sort of Minou). The big race is worth two hundred pounds. I am running a horse called Extreme Unction.

Roger

1942

1942

OFLAG VI/B

16 January
To: Mrs P. Dunne

Just received 2 December letters and will try to answer some of your inquiries. With regard to Shakespeare's sex life, I think he was an all-round sportsman and rode with equal enthusiasm under both rules. I agree with you that very sane, balanced people are usually pretty dreary, and when put in strange surroundings such as mine, are very much less adaptable. I've always been pretty mad and I doubt if I've become any odder. Of course, in a place like this, what you mentioned is certain to crop up and it is amazing how it changes people's characters. Most of them take it terribly seriously, just like a boy of eighteen having his first affair, and become very tiresome in consequence. Were you ever at a girls' school? If so, you can imagine the situations that arise. Luckily, lack of place and opportunity are a fairly good safeguard to things going too far. Have you ever read Christopher Isherwood's *Mr Norris Changes Trains*? I think it's extremely amusing: an actual Mr Norris does in fact exist and is now in prison. Our local Captain Grimes runs true to form. His first wife left him after Grimes came in tight and mistook her shoes for the WC. He has just told me a marvellous story which ended up with him being chased down Bond Street by an elderly tart in a nightdress! We had a very successful pantomime here: the 'heroine' was really disconcertingly feminine, almost frighteningly so, and Charlie Hopetoun was superb as an Ugly Sister. I am sending you a photograph (which I may have sent before) of our racing syndicate. Make some rude comments on the various members which I shall have pleasure in passing on. Have had sixty-three letters from you.

Love,
Roger

OFLAG VI/B

3 February
To: Mrs P. Dunne

I've just received your letter of 22 December. I'm afraid Peter Dollar has gone to another camp: I never spoke to him here. I hope Bob Laycock turns up: I only met him once in France some years ago and he struck me as being one of the most intelligent and broadminded officers I've ever come across. The weather here has been pleasantly cool, some forty degrees of frost. Paul quite likes his new school, although the wartime regime is spartan in the extreme. The masters are pretty strict, I believe, but the pupils treat them with an easy condescension, which I'm afraid irritates them very considerably! However, it is a very good education in the broad sense of the word. Most of us here are suffering from a serious lack of female company. I find that a letter from any girl I'm at all fond of almost makes me blub! We had a small ice rink here and I have been floundering round it, chiefly on my arse or the inside of my ankles. It is a good exercise, I suppose, but it's rather more pain than pleasure. One of my room companions, who I've lived with now for eighteen months is a bit mad in the best possible sense (he always has been). It is difficult to describe his form without making him appear a dreary professional humourist. He is seldom himself but is usually playing the part of a typical idiotic Conservative MP, a debutante, a Jew (his one great hate in life), a very old and doddery general or a somewhat oversexed parson. He is busy writing two books, his biography entitled *With*

Whip and Spur Through the West End of London and a smaller volume, *Every Man a Homo at Heart.* None of this sounds particularly amusing, but as he is a very kind and unselfish person as well, he has been a tremendous asset to our captivity. In the days of blackest depression, he just keeps us from cutting our throats.

All my love,
Roger

OFLAG VI/B

19 March
To: Mrs P. Dunne

I should like your opinion of how many wives of husbands who are prisoners of war are likely to remain absolutely 'faithful' during the period of separation. I say about 45 per cent, but idealistic and optimistic married men reckon on 85 per cent! As regards work here, I have my time nicely occupied with household chores – bed-making, book learning, darning, washing-up, cooking, etc. In the summer I garden: beyond that I do no work and I don't take on an enormous amount of violent exercise. I have just read two very enjoyable books – *Pillar To Post* by Osbert Lancaster and *USA*, a trilogy by Dos Passos, some of it is rather deliberately obscure, but I think that the rest is pretty good. The thaw has come at last and the ditches are in full flow, so there has been a brief craze for racing small chips of wood down the drains. Entry fees are ten shillings or one pound and there are often fifteen or twenty starters. About two months after I was captured, I wrote out my brief and undistinguished war experiences in a couple of notebooks: I took quite a lot of trouble about it: today I re-read them, sweated with shame and embarrassment and hastily threw them into the stove! Thank God I don't keep a diary.

I'm so glad you remember Captain Jones hunting with the Whaddon. He is a perfect representative of a certain type of person who goes through life perpetually broke, living up to an income of about two thousand pounds a year, known locally as 'the captain' and is a sort of amateur dealer. They can be found in nice profusion in the hunting field, on the polo ground and at all horse shows. Sometimes they make good like Maurice Kingscote. This is a wretched, ill-written letter.

Roger

OFLAG VI/B

4 April
To: Mrs P. Dunne

I have carefully put aside that letter you sent me 'to await arrival'. I'm sorry you're feeling so depressed: I think anyone with any feelings or imagination must often wonder whether it is worthwhile continuing with life. Sometimes circumstances combine to drag me down until you eventually tire of struggle and are prepared to slip away from it all. Usually, though, the instinct for self-preservation prevents you from doing anything more drastic than indulging in a period of very morbid self-pity. I think insomnia, love and indigestion make me more miserable than anything else. I disagree with you about Charles Morgan. I think *The Voyage* and *Portrait In A Mirror* are novels of the very best sort. On the other hand I thought *Sparkenbroke* was pretentious rot and I longed for Beachcomber, or Nervo and Knox to suddenly appear and rag it unmercifully. Some of Charles Morgan's characters worry themselves to death over going to bed with someone else and really get very tiresome about it. Frankly, I think they would do better with a trifle more action and a little less introspection. Very many thanks for the books you sent me. So far I've read *The Power And The Glory*, which is far the best thing he's written. I can think of no one, not even Aldous Huxley, who can portray pain, degradation and abysmal squalor so accurately! I'm enjoying Siegfried Sassoon's poems very much, particularly 'December Stillness', 'The Dug-Out' and 'Everyone Sang'. I think his bitterness was that of a sensitive man and a good soldier worn down by beastliness and the folly of others. My feelings here, though sympathetic to his, are a rather cheap sort of sourness caused by a feeling of personal failure and sense of humiliation.

Best love,
Roger

OFLAG VI/B

6 April
To: Mrs P. Dunne

I've just received your long letter of 1 March, asking me to give a description of myself. Before I get on to that, I wish to refer to something you wrote in the postscript. Just get it into your head that I'm no more like your friend Dollar than you're like my friend Milly. Bloody I may be, but I am certainly not so crude, so noisy or such an appalling bounder as he is. My sense of humour is the exact antithesis of his, as I am bored to tears by dirty stories which are his speciality. I very much enjoyed your comments on the photograph I sent you as it was perfectly obvious that you mistook me for Neville Usher. As he is ten years younger than I am, I don't really mind. As regards myself, I am frequently told I have 'a very bitter tongue'. This is, I'm ashamed to say, fairly true, but I make a point of not applying it to friends. I have few moral scruples but loyalty to my friends is one of them. About other people, I admit I am not particular and probably mischievous and malicious. I am extremely fond of my father but I have never been able to get on very well with my mother as our natures and outlooks are entirely incompatible. As a result, we quarrelled incessantly during my childhood and now, when we are both more tolerant, we are too shy of each other to feel happy in each other's presence. I'm bone idle, loathe late nights and parties and shooting. I'm too lazy to have many serious love affairs but have short and not unhappy ones. I worry about my health, have 'doubts'

(like Mrs Prendergast) in religion. My pleasures are reading, racing, hunting, real tennis, mobbing and being alone.
I prefer married women to single (to be continued).

Roger

1942

OFLAG VI/B

6 April
Postcard to: Mrs P. Dunne

Continuing from the letter of the same date, I dislike
possessive people with an acute sense of their own property,
hearty, jolly persons, men like the Weldon brothers, people
with an inflated sense of self entitlement, a great many
debutantes. I am very happy indeed in my regiment, many
of my friends are in it and I am quite keen on soldiering – I
like coarse jokes, Milly and most tarts. I enjoy most riding
school at about 8 a.m. on a spring morning, playing real
tennis at Lords, fooling with Ronald, reading Irish history
or modern history or just sneering at things in rather a
cheap sort of way. I dislike Wagner but am devoted to
Mozart, Beethoven and I fear Tchaikovsky.

Roger

OFLAG VI/B

18 May
To: Mrs Dunne

I hope you're all right again after that tiresome operation. I'm so glad you didn't tell me anything about it as I'm inclined to be bored by other people's illnesses, even if they are of a somewhat intimate nature. You're perfectly right, my March letter was extremely dreary. I suppose it's partly the result of being locked up in dreary surroundings during the spring. I've been reading Macaulay's critical essays: there are some very admirable phrases in them. I liked the description of a gentleman, 'whose life was divided between turgid repose and the most odious forms of sensuality'. I've also been reading a great deal about Bismarck – an admirable realist. I rather liked his statement, 'Leave to the vanquished only their eyes to weep with.' My life isn't only household chores. I've learnt quite a lot about music and quite the best evenings here are gramophone concerts in our room, selected and explained by Richard Wood. Naturally, there are many other things as well. I gave Charlie Hopetoun your message and he said some very nice things about you. Charlie is a tremendous personality and always in very good form. Another amusing character here was Wing Commander Bader who had no legs but undefeatable spirit and personality. I hope your son likes Ludgrove. I was at school at the place when it was Wixenford and was very happy there. Ronald and John Fox-S. (I'm so pleased about him) were there too. There is a master there still called Reed who I'm very fond of, and is the very best possible type of private schoolmaster.

Yours with love, repressed but cheerful. I'd love *Race-form*.

Roger

OFLAG VI/B

12 June
To: Mrs P. Dunne

Just received a very good letter from you, dated 3 May. It was extremely kind of you to write to S. S. [Siegfried Sassoon] on my behalf, as you must have felt very shifty writing off to a complete stranger. It was also very nice of him to reply as he did and I have written a postcard thanking him. I was delighted with the two very good and very disarming photographs of your children on the ice: they made me regret very much that I was a middle-aged bachelor. Why is it that little girls always ride much better than boys and are far less nervous? We had the first radishes from our room garden today: the lettuce is rather backward but the spinach is full of promise. I'm ashamed to say we have been too materialistic to indulge in flowers and quite rightly I expect you'll think the worse of us for it. Actually, we have planted a few rows of marigolds on the grave of our cat. I've been interested in Irish history ever since I used to spend the summer there nearly twenty years ago. My uncle lives in Co. Wicklow and quietly loses money at farming, breeding horses and being an MFH. I am very fond of him and his entire family and have spent a good deal of my leave there and been far happier there than anywhere else. I like the informality and the leisured pace of life there: the country is lovely and I am very fond of the people. I was very touched that the village burnt candles for me, a Protestant Englishman, when they thought I was killed!

I'm afraid it will never seem quite the same again as my cousin, David Mitchell, the only son, was killed aged twenty a year ago.

    Love,

    Roger

PS: I have *no* moustache.

OFLAG VI/B

18 June
To: Mrs P. Dunne

I think you must write very good letters as I feel compelled to answer them the moment I've read them. I've just received two, 17 and 22 May and will answer some questions. I absolutely agree with you that one's outlook depends almost entirely on one's state of health. I've always been dyspeptic and consequently somewhat sour: melancholic and pessimistic in outlook. I find the Church of England completely unsatisfactory and I think it far too much like a spiritual branch of the Conservative Party Association. If I had any strong religious feelings I should turn briskly towards Rome. I have sufficient clothing, most of which is washed and repaired by myself. I have a cold shower every morning and one hot one every week. If there were no English or German censors I could write you a really interesting letter to prove to you that prison has its moments and life is often less dull than might be supposed. Paul is surprisingly happy at school but he has a lot of friends there, which makes up for anything. Some of the masters are, I am afraid, very unpleasant indeed and from all accounts go far beyond the bounds needed in looking after young boys. I might be quite worried by it but from what I know of Paul he is capable of looking after himself. I've met Denis Atkinson – a rather pompous young man in a dim cavalry regiment. Yes, I'd love the gramophone records you kindly offer. Delighted to hear war has not destroyed your unusual looks.

    Love,
    Roger

OFLAG VI/B

17 July
To: Mrs P. Dunne

I've just received your letter of 15 June, obviously written when you were on good form. I only wish I had sufficient paper to make an adequate reply. Firstly, I received a vast number of books the other day, mostly from you. I took them off to my bed, rather like a dog taking his bone to the basket, and spent the rest of the day deciding which to read first. Eventually, I decided on *The Informer* which I've read a good many times and always enjoy. I always regret it was such a poor film, with Victor McLaglen hardly more like an Irishman than Paul Robeson or Toscanini. Have you read *The Martyrs* by Liam O'Flaherty? I don't think it's his best book, but it's one of my favourites. I don't know if you read books on modern Irish history, but two that I liked were *The Invisible Army* and *The Big Fellow*, a biography of Michael Collins. There is a very good story of a child in Dublin called *The Garden* by L. A. G. Strong: being prone to a good dollop of sentimentality, I enjoyed it almost as much as I did *Black Beauty* in my youth. I'm afraid I've fallen a victim to more or less the same little trouble as last year and will have to have ten days' rest and quiet, which makes a pleasant change and improves my temper. I can't remember off hand any records I particularly liked recently, except a concerto by César Franck with Cortot at the piano and Beethoven's No. 3, conducted by Toscanini. Very many thanks for the books: I shall now be able to indulge in more turgid repose on my bed.

Roger

OFLAG VI/B

24 August

My dear Peggy. The flower garden outside our hut has been most successful. The ground was completely bare to start with, but two large triangles of grass were planted, the sides being from twenty-five to fifty yards long. With some difficulty, people were induced not to walk on it in the spring, and the results have repaid the inconvenience. The triangles are edged with long beds of massed cornflower, poppies, marigolds, zinnias and clarkia – the cornflowers being particularly effective in a place so singularly lacking any colours but grey and brown. I had no share in this, but have had much pleasure and good results from a small vegetable patch, the young carrots and onions being a pleasant change. Like Peter Dollar, I've been resting for a bit. I read some extremely good books during that time – Rosebery's *Pitt*, Trevelyan's *History 1780-1920*, Henri Barbusse's *Under Fire*, and *Dusty Answer*. In one book I read the following and it has stuck in my mind: 'Once youth has gone, the best one can hope for is that age will blunt one's perception to the miseries of life.' You asked me why I worry about my health: I suppose because I'm introspective: anyway, I don't worry anyone else about it. I haven't got another photograph, but if you still have the dreary thing I sent you, I'm in the first row, I think on the right of the elderly officer in the centre. Give my love to John Fox-S.

Roger

Moved to

OFLAG VII B Block II

OFLAG VII B Block II

19 September
To: Mrs P. Dunne

I'm afraid I have not written for some time owing to moving to this new camp, which is in delightful surroundings and near a very charming small town. It is a welcome change after our last home. The camp itself will probably be quite adequate once we get it efficiently sorted out and organised. My only regret is that owing to my being quartered in a block reserved for those with prison 'pasts', I have had to leave my old mess with whom I've been for twenty-seven months. Luckily, one of them has come with me and we are sharing a bed and as we are in a very good mess which includes Hector Christie, who was once trainer to Lady

Lindsay; Tony Rolt, who is a motor-racing expert; Gerry Pilkington; John Cripps and Terence Pritte. Still, it is rather sad leaving one's old friends, although of course I can meet them every day. Albert, whom you asked after, is in good heart and much improved health. At some recent sports at our last camp, he put up a very determined long-distance performance and almost broke Jim Lewis' record! It is an immense relief after living in a really barren, gloomy, flat piece of country to see hills, woods, a river and a castle in the distance. The gardening has been well done and there are long beds of zinnias outside all the blocks.

Love,
Roger

OFLAG VII B Block II

8 November
To: Mrs P. Dunne

I'm so sorry not to have written for so long but I'm now allowed to write considerably less than formerly. I have only received seven letters since 1 September, and I usually used to get about six a week. Life here is rather unsettled as a number of officers and other ranks are segregated and in handcuffs. However, it's no earthly use worrying or thinking ahead: after all, the final result of the war is not in the least affected by what they choose to do to us here and that is the only thing that matters. I hope you will be seeing Albert Arkwright soon as he has most successfully got himself a long period of leave. What dreary bores we shall be if and when we ever emerge from this life of seclusion – all speaking a horrible prison argot, totally ignorant of world affairs, and full of dreary little eccentricities too dull even to come under the heading of Vice. All of us very repressed and looking extraordinarily shifty. I may have been odd before the war, but I intend to be considerably odder after it and make prison the excuse. Most prisoners' faces have altered a lot, and almost everyone has a really depressing expression now: we all look as if we'd been kept too long in a damp cellar (I don't infer that we have been kept in any cellar, damp or otherwise) but we do look as if toadstools could grow on us anywhere. Lack of sexual outlet was not really very worrying after the first six months, except in one or two exceptional cases, who found a substitute in what are known as perfect prison friendships – foolish but quite harmless!

Roger

OFLAG VII B Block II

30 November
To: Mrs P. Dunne

Snowing hard here and extremely cold. I've just had two letters from you full of interesting little bits. I'm so sorry Ronald appears to be behaving badly to Zara: he's not really a suitable type for marriage – far too intolerant and his contempt for women is seldom concealed for long. He ought to have married someone as odd as himself, fairly insensitive, and with immense capacity for management and discipline – a sort of nursery governess with limited sex appeal. I hardly know Parker Bowles but I dislike him a great deal without the slightest justification. I always thought his wife was very attractive but likely to become a second edition of his mother. I had my birthday last week and we had a small party: dinner for twenty followed by some mild gambling – nothing very exciting but it was a change and great fun. I hope old Portobello wins a race or two before the end of the season. I have a certain amount of affection for him, having opposed him in both his Ascot races in 1939 and had a good win on him at Newmarket. Bellamoun sounds very useful as I imagine it takes a good two-year-old to win any sort of race these days. Is Bellacose getting many winners? I have decided to go and live quietly in Ireland after the war, and start life more or less afresh. In actual fact, I shall probably, if I'm lucky, get some dreary little job in London and live in a temperance lodging house in the Cromwell Road.

Roger

OFLAG VII B Block II

31 December
To: Mrs P. Dunne

I have just received with great delight Fisher's *European History* which you sent me about eighteen months ago. Thank you so much, a better prison book could not be imagined. The gramophone records and some books that you so kindly sent me about five months ago have not arrived yet but, like everything else, I feel sure they'll arrive in good time. Our room has just been distempered and I chose a very pale yellow, with a grass-green line round the top. It is a warm sort of colour and gives the illusion of sunlight; at any rate it has made quite a difference to the combined bedroom, pantry, larder, kitchen, dining room where, with seventeen others, I pass twenty-three hours out of twenty-four. People are much easier to live with than they used to be, and I hope I am too. Communal life is a tremendous art based on experience and a tolerance which the experience brings with it. We live in our room in one mess with everything shared, which smooths out most petty squabbles and gives one more incentive to carry out the endless room chores. The general tone of the room is hard to describe: but no one is allowed to take anything seriously and such things as one's religion, parents, regiment, war experiences, come in for pretty severe chi-hiking – in fact anything that one was never allowed to rag people about at school. We all think ourselves amazingly cynical and amusing whereas in actual fact we're very childish and sour about our own failures. Ludgrove's a nice place on the whole. I enjoyed myself very much when it was Wixenford.

Best love,
Roger

1943

1943

OFLAG VII/B Block II

5 January
Postcard to: Mrs P. Dunne

I have just received your letter of 4 November and felt I must write at once and tell you how very sorry I am to hear about your mother and I can only pray that there will be no long drawn-out period of suffering. A great friend of mine, Tony Lawrence, died of cancer a few years ago when he was only twenty-six, so that in some small degree I can realise what your feelings are now.

   Roger

OFLAG VII/B Block II

14 January
Postcard to: Mrs P. Dunne

The gramophone records that you so kindly sent me last summer have arrived, and I can only congratulate you on having made a very good choice and tell you that they have given considerable pleasure here to a large number of people. I particularly liked the piano concerto and preferred it considerably to Toscanini and Horowitz who is just a bit too slick sometimes. Many thanks.

Roger

OFLAG VII B Block II

10 February
To: Mrs P. Dunne

I've just had a letter you wrote on 26 December and I'll try and answer some questions. I'm very well after a fairly unpleasant week with an abscess on a tooth and another complaint which is very common, very unromantic, and very painful and entailing most humiliating treatment. I've been very steady and domesticated this winter – plenty of housemaid's work interspersed by a great deal of reading. I've particularly enjoyed Gibbon's *Decline And Fall*, Macaulay's *History Of England*; Morley's *Life Of Gladstone*, Garvais' *Joseph Chamberlain* and Evelyn Waugh's *Put Out More Flags*. Also two books I feel sure you would like, *The Croquet Player* and *Mr Britling*, both by H. G. Wells. To improve my German, I'm laboriously translating *Alice In Wonderland*. Frankly, I doubt if my version would convey to a German much sense of the original. Have you ever read a book called the *Way Of Revelation*? It is by Wilfrid Ewart, who was in the Scots Guards and was murdered in Mexico some years ago. In many ways, I think it is one of the best war novels in existence. Mentally, I feel better than at any time since 1939. I think prison has done me very little harm and some good. I am now far better read, far less smug and conceited, far more tolerant and considerably more capable of looking after myself. I have had ample time to sit down and think what an awful bloody fool I've been in the past, and how I've wasted time, money and opportunities. I don't grudge the money a bit, but I do grudge the time now I'm growing middle-aged. I'm very happy in my associates here and hope many of them will remain my friends after release. On the debit side, I've lost what little religion I had and my outlook (like that of most failures) is full of sneers and bitterness. One thing I have learnt – when times are really hard and difficult, the veneer of birth, education, etc. is shown to be amazingly thin.

Love,
Roger

OFLAG VII B Block II

4 March
Postcard to: Mrs P. Dunne

I'm afraid I've been giving the wrong impression, as I'm not in chains. Life here has improved a lot since I wrote that dreary letter and I am as happy as possible in these circumstances. The chained people don't have at all a bad time and they don't wear them in bed or to go to the lavatory, a point which appeared to be puzzling you. By the way, I've always wondered how Amy Johnson managed in her long flights and Captain Scott at the North Pole. Come for a month to Germany with me after the war. It's a lovely country.

Roger

OFLAG VII B Block II

2 April
Postcard to: Mrs P. Dunne

Sorry I haven't written for over a month but for some time past, I've been under a cloud and have had to rest by myself. In spite of advancing age, I feel pathetically full of spring feeling: as you can imagine, there is no outlet here for any seasonal urge that one may happen to possess. I hear that there is going to be an Ascot meeting this year: I do hope old Portobello will win there. I'd give my ears for just one day at Newmarket.

    Love,
    Roger

OFLAG VII B Block II

20 April
To: Mrs P. Dunne

I'm pleased to hear that some of my letters have turned up at last. Yours always get here in the long run, although in the most extraordinary sequence. I'm glad you write about yourself – yours are almost the only letters I get that I can't pretty well guess the contents of before I read. In prison, where time means less than nothing, one can indulge oneself in extremely pleasant sedentary occupations; for the last two days, I've sat all day watching two goldfinches just outside my room – a simple pleasure but one I've never had enough leisure for before. We get a lot of fun out of our actors here: they shoot a tremendous phoney line about art for art's sake and sacrificing their leisure to entertain the camp. In actual fact, they take up more room then they're worth, squabble hideously over their parts, show off their dreary temperaments, and usually only provide the dingiest type of amateur theatricals. If one criticises the performers, one is either completely blind to real art or an ungrateful swine! Frankly, I'm afraid I must be both. Today's the sort of day that makes me homesick – warm and wet, with rain dripping off the leaves, and everything very green and new. I've always been very much against PT, and a few days ago Peter Dodd in the next room did some, and just sat down and died afterwards, poor devil. I've just heard a very good record – Elisabeth Schumann singing 'Bist Du Bei Mir'.

Love,
Roger

OFLAG VII B Block II

9 May
Postcard to: Mrs P. Dunne

Just a short note of apology for having sent a somewhat tactless communication a month or two ago. It was extremely thoughtless of me but I feel sure your prestige is sufficiently well-founded to prevent it tottering as a result of some rather elementary crudeness on my part. I'm cook (temporarily thank God!) and feel about whacked after hacking up some spinach and pounding up stale crusts and broken biscuits with a chair leg to form the basis of some thick tomato sauce.

    Roger

OFLAG VII B Block II

31 May
To: Mrs P. Dunne

Your mention of Liam O'Flaherty's book, *Mr Gilhooley*, made me remember my intense fury when my house tutor confiscated it when he found me reading it in bed one night. I think I was about fifteen at the time, and had expended seven and sixpence on the book in the hope that it would prove to be extremely indecent. Mr Gilhooley, if my memory is correct, slightly intoxicated, had just climbed into bed with a very low class of woman, and a fairly detailed description of what followed was unfortunately interrupted by the confiscation of the book. I haven't read anything very exciting recently but enjoyed *The Second Embrace* by Philip Guedalla and Trevelyan's *Garibaldi*. I hardly ever read a novel, not from any choice of mine, but because it is almost impossible to send modern novels out here. But I read *The Lunatic At Large* for the first time, also some good steady Victorian books on hunting by the Druid and by the hunting correspondent of *The Field* 1890-1900. They seemed to have tremendous sport with the Warwickshire in those days. It's a little depressing reading history – the same mistakes over and over again, the old lessons never learned, and the human race not merely imperfect, but perennially foolish and often criminal and beastly as well. Christianity, unfortunately, has not the slightest influence in world problems, but I cannot see any settled prospect for the years to come unless there is a great religious revival throughout Europe. But even if that took place, people would soon start fighting over their dreary dogmas and creeds as they've always done in the past.

Best love,
Roger

OFLAG VII B Block II

4 July
Postcard to: Mrs P. Dunne

I'm awfully sorry I didn't write last month but life has been very dingy here, as most of my friends have been sent to other camps, while things haven't been going too well at home either. I'm so sorry to hear about your mother and can only hope that there was no suffering. I'm more depressed and lonely than I've ever been before. I'm nothing like as mentally tough as I was, and prison without one's friends is about the end.

Roger

OFLAG VII B Block II

14 July
Postcard to: Mrs P. Dunne

How short your memory is! My postcard of apology was in reply to a sharp diplomatic protest from you, that a very crude postcard from me which concerned certain aspects of voyages to the Pole and Amy Johnson's flights had sullied your spotless local reputation. That seems a very clumsy sentence, but I'm in hospital with sinus trouble and my head aches like hell.

    Best love,
    Roger

OFLAG VII B Block II

1 August
To: Mrs P. Dunne

It is amazingly hot here, but as I'm in bed and can't get out it merely increases my sense of frustration. I've just re-read two of my favourite books – *Anna Karenina* and Sassoon's *Fox-Hunting Man*. Frankly, I couldn't live more than a fortnight with any of Tolstoy's women – they spend their entire time in raptures of passion or floods of tears – an exceedingly tiring combination. Have you seen Ronald lately? He's only written to me once since I've been in prison so I'm completely out of touch with him. We shall meet again as two complete strangers – one a down-at-heel, shifty, shambling ex-convict, the other perhaps a stoutish, baldish, smug family man. By God I'm sorry for his infants if he has to look after them ever on nurse's night out. On the whole, I rather like children except for the following ages – both sexes up to four, boys between nine and fourteen, girls between thirteen and seventeen. My liking is qualified by the fact that they should have a good strict nurse as governess always at hand to remove them if they're tiresome. What I cannot stand are first-year debutantes, and undergraduates. It's very odd how many people turn Roman Catholic in prison. Can you account for it?

    Love,
    Roger

OFLAG VII B Block II

31 August
To: Mrs P. Dunne

Well, here I am at the end of my fourth summer in prison – physically somewhat more bent and decrepit, mentally a great deal more childish, but on the whole not much to grumble about and if needs be I daresay I could do another four. I was delighted to hear you were making a big hit with a charming American – I think you'd had a depressing time lately and something like that will do you good. I can't think about what I'm going to do when I get home – I should like to get some job on the police, something connected with racing but I expect I shall end up as something really dreary. If I could afford it I think I'd retire quietly and live in a cottage on the west coast of Ireland. If we've any money after the war, let's take a motor and go up through central Europe and the Balkans for a few months. I've been reading a good deal about that part of the world lately and I believe we could have a good time there. Did you send me some amusing short stories from the magazine *Horizon*? If so, I enjoyed them a lot, particularly that very horrible little Spanish story called 'The Scissors'. I've been reading some *Prejudices* by H. L. Mencken – good, powerful, vulgar invective directed chiefly against the evangelical church and God knows they deserve it. Well done, old Portobello!

Best love,
Roger

OFLAG VII B Block II

3 September
To: Mrs P. Dunne

In your last letter, you ask me whether I want you to go on writing. Quite honestly, I should be very lost without your letters now, you are almost the only person I hear from whose letters aren't a series of drab, commonplace mixed up with a few sops in the shape of foolish optimism – I've been told 'next Christmas' since August 1940! As long as you can stand it, please go on – until you've been in prison you can't possibly realise what letters mean; in the first year or so, most of us used to get written to a lot; now, in the fourth year, the number has decreased tremendously, which is perfectly natural, as people have other things to think of, more work to do, and at any rate, our existence is probably completely forgotten by now. Thank you very much for 'Princess Lieven' – in her picture she looks rather unattractive, in fact pert and inquisitive, but as old Metternich (who was no mean judge) bedded down with her, she must have had considerable charm. Frankly, I should have found her rather alarming, although with her great political flair she could always make herself interesting. I've just read Brogan's *Republican France 1870–1939*, extremely good and very amusing and easy to read. Can I come and stay with you for a few days after the war? You'll be able to tell me everything that's happened, and I think I could enlighten you a bit, too.

Love,
Roger

OFLAG VII B Block II

4 November
Postcard to: Mrs P. Dunne

I had three letters from you yesterday – I'm awfully sorry I didn't write last month but I intended to write on the 31st but I heard the day before that John Loyd, my greatest friend, had died very suddenly of TB on returning from Africa, and I had to write to his family. I wish you'd known him – an extraordinarily 'good' person without being in any way a prig, tolerant and quick-witted and the best sense of fun I've ever known. He was one of the few people who had Ronald tied up in a string bag!

   Roger

OFLAG VII B Block II

10 November
To: Mrs P. Dunne

I do hope you're still having a fairly good time and you see plenty of your American friend. I can tell from your letter that you're in better form than you've been for years. I'm living in a pleasant room for ten – almost all of us are dreary old things between the ages of thirty and thirty-four, all of us captured three and a half years ago. We get on extraordinarily well together, having learnt by experience the art of communal living – we all have our peculiarities and danger points – Lee Windsor gets furious if any remark is made about big heads or premature baldness, Micky Smiley doesn't like losing at piquet (who does, for that matter?), Parky Goucus is driven frantic by the Church of England, and surplus optimism makes me see red. Of course it isn't so much fun as the last room I was in where life was a cross between a Marx Brothers film and a Nervo and Knox act: but non-stop buffoonery might have become tiring after a year, although it sharpened one's wits, because if you ever let up for a moment and said anything foolish, smug, or patently untrue, it was brought home to you in a most wounding fashion. We're much more sedate here, and on the whole, behave more in accordance with our age. There are a lot of people in this camp who are extraordinarily nice, and the tendency is, strangely enough, to like people very much more nowadays than one did a year or so ago. This is the pleasantest camp I've yet been in for many reasons and I keep reasonably happy with spells of depression.

Best love,
Roger

OFLAG VII B Block II

20 December
Postcard to: Mrs P. Dunne

Very best wishes and love for the new year and very many thanks for your unfailing kindness to me during the past three and a half years, a period which you have made considerably less drab than it might have been otherwise. I've got a sudden craze for theological philosophy, but find my slender knowledge makes me easy prey for cultured Catholics and earnest atheists. I remember, though, Mr Prendergast's warning: 'Lay interest in purely ecclesiastical matters is so often a prelude to insanity!'

    Roger

1944

1944

OFLAG VII B Block II

2 January
To: Mrs P. Dunne

I've had a busy and comparatively enjoyable week – a visit to the local cinema where I saw a German film in colour – *Baron Munchausen* – which was remarkably good. Last night I went to our own pantomime which always makes me sick with laughter. I'm afraid though that some of the 'girls' are getting a bit part-worn after four years 'inside'. Best of all I had a two-hour walk in the woods on my own and felt almost human once more. Unfortunately, I'm incurably introspective, as I believe you are too and that inevitably leads to long periods of doubt, mistrust, and ultimate unhappiness. I think it's partly a physical condition, but then one's whole outlook on life is dictated by the state of one's stomach. I went to church last week, the first time for two years – I had the greatest difficulty in not letting my thoughts wander on to every kind of improbable and undesirable topic. How bloody for you having insomnia – I had it for a short time some years ago and more or less overcame it by having a really stodgy meal late in the evening, swilled down with Guinness and port. I then went to bed at once in a warm room with the windows shut and usually passed out fairly quickly, and remained out till the next morning.

Best love,
Roger

OFLAG VII B Block II

24 January
Postcard to: Mrs P. Dunne

No, I'm not surprised to hear that R. is commanding a battalion. I think he is certain to do it very well; he has astonishing self-confidence for that sort of thing, as well as ample courage. I've just been talking to Jocelyn Abel-Smith, whose offspring is also at Ludgrove, and is apparently very happy there. I myself had a much happier time there than I ever did at Eton. I've smugly decided that prison has improved me – and consider myself – probably without justification – more tolerant, far kinder, less libellous and malicious, better educated, and far humbler, in fact a bloody little prig!

   Roger

OFLAG VII B Block II

31 January
To: Mrs P. Dunne

The first day of spring, really warm, and I've been out all day splitting tree roots for pinewood by driving steel wedges in. Even what little blood there is in my crackling old arteries felt slightly stirred, so I suppose my senses are not yet completely atrophied. I heard from one of the repatriated prisoners the other day, and he said what struck him most was how small women were! I have only spoken to a woman once in the last three and a half years – when I had the good fortune to have a tooth stopped by a most charming and efficient woman dentist. The combined effect of being both a prisoner and totally unused to female company was to make me feel appallingly gauche and adolescent. We're all arguing fiercely about the Beveridge plan here – almost everyone is in favour of it, except for a few reactionary landowners, and of course, R.C.s, who are always scared stiff of social reform. I've read a lot lately, *The Life of Lord Haldane* (one of those very rare creatures, an honest and effective statesman), *The Unknown God* by Alfred Noyes, Foch's *Principles De Guerre*, and *The Age of Reform* by Woodward. Have you read *The Eccentricities of Cardinal Perelli*, by Ronald Firbank? Life here isn't at all bad at present – it's by far the best camp I've been in, and time passes quickly. I hope Matron has by now ceased to be the heaviest cross in your life. Best love and many thanks for your letters,
    Roger

OFLAG VII B Block II

29 February
To: Mrs P. Dunne

I read with interest about your visit to Mr de Q. (about whom I read in agricultural papers from time to time). I was discussing it later with Jack Poole who said he knew him a bit, and was at school with him. He thinks Q. is somewhat 'peculiar', and I rather fancy from your description that you would agree, although you would scarcely be in the position to find out! Jack Leslie, who lives in our room, told me this (Jack is the son of Shane L. who is Irish, R.C. and imaginative; and writes amusing books): 'Old Lady Tredegar, now aged about eighty, every year in the spring gets an urge to make birds' nests. She makes them – chiefly wrens' and hedge sparrows' – in various somewhat inconvenient corners all over the house; specimens have been sent to the British Museum who cannot distinguish them from the work of birds – a thing absolutely without precedent. Furthermore, I believe her son looks like a bird.' How do you account for it all? Now there is one thing I am anxious to know. Has the social order in England completely vanished? Are hunting, big houses, Ascot, the 'privileged' class mere memories of the past? I was pleased to hear your optimistic views about the war for myself. I have no particular views: when I was captured I set myself to do four years. I shall be lucky if I get away with five.

Best wishes,
Roger

OFLAG VII B Block II

31 March
To: Mrs P. Dunne

Many thanks for at least five letters in ten days. I am taking a grave risk in sending you a photograph of myself to prove that life is not yet extinct. From left to right, Jack Leslie, Irish Guards, a delightful person who thinks all day of ghosts, fairies and the past and is never quite on this Earth. Next, Micky Smiley, Rifle Brigade, who luckily for him and for us doesn't look as sour and as gross as he appears here: he is an MFH in Sussex and married one of the numerous Pearson girls (Lavinia). He was a great friend of mine at Eton and the RMC. Behind him is Michael Price, 'the prawn'; he thoroughly enjoys mild ill-health, having once broken his back in a race. He is a good-natured butt. Then Fitz Fletcher, 'The Rook', who is very reserved, smooth and polite and comes from Meath. He was up at Cambridge when the war started and like many reserved people, is, I believe, successful in 'love'. He is a thoroughly nice person (as indeed they all are). The raddled old scarecrow propped against the wall is myself, wearing a self-knitted hat, a coat from America, and a pair of boots sent me by an R. C. bishop. The spring won't come here; it is still snowing hard today. I've only one print of this photograph; could you be very kind and send it to my father?

  Best love,
  Roger

OFLAG VII B Block II

23 May
To: Mrs P. Dunne

I was very glad to hear from you again yesterday after a long interval due to a hold-up in the mail. I consider your report on the new social order was a masterpiece – tense but extraordinarily illuminating. On Sunday morning at 9.15, a thousand of us trooped off to a special performance given to us by a travelling circus! It was really most amusing and a very pleasant change to see a female acrobat and contortionist after four years of hideous male bodies, all too frequently exposed either in the nude or at moments that should be strictly private. I've been for one or two good walks lately up in the woods overlooking the river and I've really felt frighteningly Geoffrey Winnish watching the sun come through the beech trees on to the masses of lilies of the valley below. As a rule, I loathe playing cards for money, I find it so boring, but the Canadians here have instituted a game called 'Black Jack' which is first rate. I play every evening now for amounts which I would never have dreamt of in England. I haven't read much lately; I've had my annual go at the *Diary Of A Nobody*, and I've also read a most interesting book by a London magistrate, John Watson, called *The Child and the Magistrate*. By the way, how is that spirit of brisk optimism that you showed at Christmas? Not dwindling away, I hope.

    Love,
    Roger

OFLAG VII B Block II

30 June
To: Mrs P. Dunne

I have got a knitting craze for the moment: yesterday I ran up rather a pansy little white tie out of the sleeve of an old tennis sweater, and today I'm fumbling feverishly away at a three-strand sweater for myself using the unexpended portion of some caggy old socks for the wool. Some new prisoners arrived last week: frankly I find them a little tiresome as a rule: they're either patronisingly sympathetic to us old deadbeats or else they bullshit most aggressively about the war. I haven't read much lately except a textbook called *The Greek View of Life* which is fairly heavy weather. By the way, two of the new inmates are very welcome: one plays brass wind instruments in the London Philharmonic Orchestra and another is a pianist in a dance band. Are you satisfied with Bellacose's stud achievements to date? I suppose that it takes a good sort of horse to win any kind of race nowadays, and the opportunities for two-year-olds not quite in the top class are few and far between. I'm afraid that with so few horses in training, there are almost too many Hyperions and Blue Peters. Do you ever see Nigel Courage nowadays? It's a long time since I used to make a fairly indifferent job of bandaging his leg every morning (until, rightly, I was sacked from my job as hospital assistant!).

Roger

OFLAG VII B Block II

My dear Peggy,

Many thanks for your letters. How's old Portobello? I've always hoped to see him win the last race at the first Ascot after the war. You asked me if I had developed any political views – well I have – of a sort. I don't think any particular political party attracts me much. I rather prefer the Labour Party for home affairs but their ideas of foreign policy have always shown an almost contemptible lack of realism. I suppose the ideal statesman is the idealist who realises what can be accomplished in his own generation. Personally, I welcome any scheme for social security provided the country as a whole is made aware of its obligations as well, such as military service. Between the last two wars, we all got deplorably soft and any idea of service to the country was regarded as reactionary and tyrannical. I think that point of view will die down with the gradual disappearance of the small, privileged governing class that has made such a mess of things in the past, and if equal educational opportunities are provided, there will be a far bigger educated class from which the rulers of the country will eventually emerge. At present, too many come from the public schools and up to the age of twenty, they never come into contact with the working class at all, except for domestic servants. Do you think sour old Gibbon was right when he wrote, 'History is but the catalogues of the crimes, follies, and misfortunes of mankind'? If I had another fifteen pages I could explain myself properly. Luckily for you I haven't.

Roger

Postscript

Reading through these letters and arranging them in the correct order has been a far more moving experience than I'd bargained for.

It is hard to imagine just how bleak the outlook must have been, being a POW immediately following the military catastrophe of Dunkirk, and how low morale was. Yet my father somehow kept his sense of proportion and humour, bolstered by friends he made along the way who, in many cases, remained friends for life. There was no 'poor me' more 'things could be so much worse'. I feel I know my father rather better now and have a lot of respect for his conduct under the most challenging of circumstances. It is also extremely depressing reading about all the young, in some cases very young, men being killed in action (in particular my twenty-year-old cousin David Mitchell).

In common with many other men of his generation my father seldom talked about being a prisoner of war and on the odd occasion he did it was cushioned by his humour.

Nevertheless, I clearly remember in 1966, I was then 14, driving across the border into Germany with him on a family holiday in Baden Baden. As he reached into his briefcase to hand over our passports to the border guard for inspection, I could clearly see he was visibly shaking. Of course I never mentioned it, but it has stuck with me ever since.

The other thing that has struck me, given that my father was only in his early thirties at the time, was his humanity and wisdom. Observations such as: 'it's a little depressing reading history – the same mistakes over and over again, the old lessons never learned, and the human race not merely imperfect, but perennially foolish and often criminal and beastly as well' or 'one thing I've learnt – when times are really hard and difficult, the veneer of birth, education etc. is shown to be amazingly thin.' It also amused me that despite his sagacity on worldly matters, from time to time he could come out with some rather less profound generalisations. Debutantes in particular were a recurring theme: 'they're practically all the most shocking bores and only enjoy doing the dullest possible things. I'd sooner have the toothache than take out the average debutante.' It also made me laugh that, despite his other pet bugbear being Scotland, he was savvy enough, because Peggy was Scottish (neé Walker), not to impart his views to her on the subject as he did in a letter to his father in 1941: 'There are far too many Scotsmen in this camp. They really are the world's dreariest race, the result I suppose of a lifetime spent in damp granite hovels in the Highlands.'

My father's heart belonged to Ireland. 'My uncle lives in Co. Wicklow and quietly loses money at farming, breeding horses and being an MFH. I am very fond of him and his entire family and have been far happier there than anywhere else. The country is lovely and I am very fond of the people. If I could afford it I think I'd retire quietly and live in a cottage on the west coast of Ireland.' He was also something of an expert on Irish history and subsequently had huge sympathy with their plight at the hands of the English.

Since I started putting this book together, I have frequently thought what my father might have made of the current political shenanigans. He was not keen on what he described as 'bogus heroic stuff' (i.e. token patriotism) which he said 'was so eagerly lapped up by a large proportion of that unlovely object – the general public'. Taking that and his general tolerance and worldliness into account, I am certain that my father would have been staunchly pro-European, whereas my dear mother, who had an altogether more excitable and confrontational style, especially after a couple of large Martinis, would have taken to the streets with a pitchfork determined 'to take back control!'

In March 1943, my father wrote to Peggy: 'Come for a month to Germany with me after the war. It's a lovely country.' Given the exceptional circumstances he was in at the time, these were hardly the musings of a 'Little Englander'. A few years after the war ended my parents, who met and married in 1946, invited some Germans over for lunch on Christmas Day. My grandmother walked out in disgust . . .

More Stray Bats From An Old Belfry,
Or, Rambling Recollections
Of Life At Barclay House

[*These are personal recollections my father gave me in 1967 when we moved from our family home Barclay House, Yateley to our new home Budds Farm, Burghclere*]

We arrived at Barclay House in glorious autumn weather at the end of October 1950.

I was forty, Cynthia twenty-nine and Jane about twenty months old. We were full of hope and short of money. I think our relations thought we were insane to move here from Launceston Place.

We undertook a good deal of decoration, carried out by the friendly and totally unbusinesslike Cyril Bunch, who later lapsed inevitably and unresistingly into bankruptcy. The dining room was where the drawing room is now.

We had no money to decorate the present dining room, which was used as a box room. The Kebles must have been permanently constipated as there was a dire shortage of loos and I had one installed downstairs. There was a half-circle of grass in front of the house with an oval flower bed. I persevered with this for some years but, as Nancy McLaren invariably drove her car over it on departure, I eventually abolished it.

Behind the house there were rose pergolas and small beds outside the greenhouse. Where the herbaceous border flourishes today, there was a narrow bed containing drab annuals. Under the house on the north side there were tobacco plants and a couple of sparse shrubs. There was also a bed alongside the hedge on the left of the greenhouse.

The kitchen garden had been poorly maintained and the paths were grassed over with weeds. There was, though, an asparagus bed, subsequently uprooted and utterly destroyed by a cross-eyed, jobbing gardener known inappropriately as the 'Merry Mason'. I never loved him after that act of vandalism.

It took me two years of unremitting labour to restore order in the kitchen garden. The lower lawn remained uncut for five years, except around the edges and down the centre. I then had the grass cut and hired a small steam roller to level it down, after which we could play croquet of a sort and some infantile cricket.

At one stage, I had four dahlia beds on the lower lawn; at another, the bottom border was crammed with annuals. I created the shrub border that runs alongside the boundary between us and the White House. In the winter it used to take me weeks to tidy up that particular border.

I was mad about gardening in those days, and very igno-rant. I would happily work, even in vile winter weather, from dawn to dusk. Due to inexperience, much of my labour was futile.

In one year, we had potatoes in the smaller of the two fields. Once we grew arum lilies in the greenhouse. They did well and would have graced a rich man's funeral.

A remarkable horticultural achievement was the moving of the willow tree when its roots were found to be pene-trating the drains, with the unhappy result that sewage and loo paper had an unseemly habit of coming up on the surface of the lawn. Before Charlie Paice put us on the mains, the cesspits were emptied at irregular intervals by a man from Hartley Wintney with a birthmark on his face.

Trees, particularly unreliable elms, have crashed from time to time and, early on, some elms crashed into the Colls' garden, causing damage for which the insurance company fortunately paid up.

The garden has never been spectacular or particularly successful by standards loftier than the lowest, but for years it was my hobby and my occupational therapy, too. I loved it rather more than it deserved and gave it time that might have been applied more advantageously to alternative pursuits. I have done best with vulgar, common things, like dahlias and annuals. We had superb nectarines when we came here, but not one after some hideously inexpert pruning. A bumper crop of greengages was followed by the lingering death of that particular tree. Except for very occasional good years, our fruit trees have been just about the least productive of any in the south of England. Eventually, I paid a large sum for allegedly expert pruning and spraying. That was the final straw: the trees have been unrelentingly barren ever since.

Gardeners: Colonel Lunham, of the White House, used to mow the lawn for one pound a time. His wife strongly disapproved of this. For several years we had Cordery, who looked like a costive tortoise and whose wife, about four foot high, rode a tricycle. Cordery sometimes brought his father, born in 1865. Cordery senior told me that his mother saw the Wellington monument, en route for Heckfield, pulled through Reading by twenty-four horses and that the Reading bridge had to be shored up to take the weight.

Cordery, a very bad gardener, took umbrage over some trifling criticism and departed, to be succeeded by an even worse gardener – the Merry Mason. Then came a dishonest Irishman; the hairy-chested and agreeable Carmineri; a handsome man who worked at Toni's and disappeared without a trace, and the admirable and trustworthy Williams of the Blackbush fire brigade. He was not a great gardener but a marvellous odd-job man and a good friend to us all. He is now almost head of the fire services in Hong Kong. Charles once almost scalped Master Williams in the garden and then denied the offence with such vigour that his mother believed him, although nobody else did, of course.

After Williams was Claridge, a foul-mouthed, bibulous old reprobate who suffered alternatively from piles and diarrhoea. He had been in trouble for doing something unspeakable to a cat. He was a bad gardener with a penchant for disfiguring my best shrubs with secateurs. For some years now, we have had 'Mr Oram', alias 'Andy Capp', an indolent man little hampered by the possession of moral scruples, but rather likeable all the same.

Indoor staff: I cannot pretend to call the roll with any accuracy. Ingrid, a kindly, indolent German, was joined by her sister, Waldtraut, a less kind and more indolent type. For years, Mrs Childs was our friend and standby, and we have been assisted, too, by the soft-hearted and bird-brained Hilda. Mrs Childs was here when Charles was born and her theme song has always been 'Charlie is my Darling'. There was the gigantic Miss Barbara Shimmans, daughter of Sergeant-Major 'Bull' Shimmans; a Danish girl who annoyed Cynthia and loved a coal-black cadet from Sandhurst; the voluble and loveable Fernanda, whose romances with Major Barnett and Ron form a saga of their own; the refined and attractive Tony was mildly shocked when I gave her (why?) some sexy black knickers; a barmy Spaniard who ate raw eggs and was removed under heavy sedation; a nasty little Spaniard who sulked and then walked out on us; a gloomy Italian who only showed animation when I walked in and found her naked in the bath; the cheerful and good-natured Marian, who kept us all smiling and good-tempered; Mrs Young was for years a loyal and invaluable daily and, more recently, we have had Miss Cottrell, a rich mine for Yateley gossip, and Mrs Welton.

Happy memories of Barclay House: the births of Charles (I was in Liverpool and shall always remember Cynthia telling me on the telephone) and of Louise: Miss Reid-Scott helped to produced Charles. Miss Samways assisted at the production of Louise. I remember with particular pleasure Jane's recovery from peritonitis; Turpin; family picnics; walks with Cynthia; meeting my father at Camberley station with the children; the Christmas lunches at Hartletts; family holidays abroad; the superb childrens' parties Cynthia gave; Charles's sports party, when he was at Mallock's; his gambling party when Master Samuel soon won all the money; the parties for the Old Cold-streamers; Charles's christening when the vicar forgot the words of the service; Aunt Phylis staying for Ascot and always cutting off the lupin heads; hanging the Christmas cards; the day Phil Drake, backed at 50/1 by me, won the Derby.

Bad times: the deaths of Cynthia's father and mother and of my father; the morning Turpin was run over; Jane's illness; my own illness in 1955 when I overestimated the amount of work that I could do; Cynthia with pneumonia; the long martyrdom of our dear friend Marjorie Willett. The death of our good friends Mr Lee and Mr Butcher, of Elizabeth King, and of one of our first friends here, Admiral Hawkesley; the death of Fred, a loyal servant and friend of my father-in-law.

Turpin must head the list of our animals. Very common and entirely lovable, he was the most faithful of friends. It was a lucky day for him and us when we bought him from Battersea Dogs' Home. He very much enjoyed visiting Charles at Wellesley House. Perhaps some of our happiness and luck vanished the morning he was killed.

There were many cats, some horrid hamsters that mated in the wastepaper basket and ate Cynthia's leather coat, and some guinea pigs massacred by Pongo. I must not forget the ponies – Wendy, Rupert and Jester – that gave Cynthia so much pleasure.

Doctors: we started with Dr Russell, a trim, military figure who bred bull terriers. We later discovered he had only been in practice for a short time after retiring from the

Indian army. He died of a heart attack after flu. We then had the ineffable Dr Price, who represented the National Health Service at its most detestable. Since 1955 we have had Drs Hadfield and Whittingham. The former, who looks like a rather untidy schoolboy, has been a wonderful friend to us all, and so has the slower, more phlegmatic Dr Whittingham, with his cauliflower ears and cheerful German wife.

Schools: I look back with nostalgia to the days of Miss Tyler (five guineas a term, stationery included). Then Waverly (shades of Miss Molyneux and the tiresome Adams girls); Major Mallock's school at Fleet where Charles was happy and was reproved for repeating mildly improper rhymes*; the hideous journeys to Jane's school at Fleet with Carolin Lloyd inclined to be spiteful and Kate Collingwood tough and unpleasant. The long, bumpy, Daneshill drive; the fearful trek (all too rarely undertaken by me) to Wellesley House. Five years of trips to the convent and the inaudible carol concerts there. Mr Crawley, friend of and tutor to Charles. The children's friends – David Collett, Susan Molyneux, Carolin Lloyd, Michael Nicholson, Jamie Ponsonby, James Staples and his sisters, the two Steward boys, Charles Hurt, Helen Blair, Paul Majendie, Stephen and David Willett.

Parties: Cynthia gave marvellous children's parties and the infinite trouble she took in entertaining for the children always produced admirable results. I can see the dining-room tables loaded with food and the Charlie Chaplin films afterwards. Charles's sports party where

---

* 'O lady of Spain I adore you, so pull down your knickers and let me explore you!

lanky Michael Nicholson won all the prizes and I took the Fleet taxi driver for one of the more distinguished parents. I remember a noisy dance for Jane at Eversley Hall, firework parties – at one of which rockets nearly scalped some guests – Louise's farewell party for convent friends. Our Ascot champagne and strawberry parties with Mr Beaumont in attendance.

Friends: after the age of forty, one cannot make friends as one did in one's youth. Peter and Marjorie Willett were my best friends at Yateley.

Days I cannot forget: when Cynthia put her foot through a glass door, and the body of that poor child was found on the common. The awful drive with that mad Spanish woman to a registry office on the far side of London. A picnic with the children on a perfect September afternoon at Pottenham pond; hide-and-seek afterwards. Happy, happy days.

Cars: the Alvis 'luxury load-carrier' – a real pig: the second-hand Vauxhall bought from the Frog; flash and unreliable second-hand Jaguar, also bought from the Frog; a dull Austin Westminster; Willy Wolseley; the big Fiat which I deeply loved; the little Fiat I ran into a tree; Cynthia's Mini and Millman Minx; Charles's old wrecks that he dove insanely around the field.

Our friends Mr Brewer and Mr Wells, and Charles's friend Mr Blackman. A good friend who died all too young: Didi Sutherland. An outstanding flop: Charles's cricket lessons at Sunningdale.

Days I really hated: Charles off to Wellesley House. How quiet the house used to seem without him and how Cynthia and I loved having him home.

Good holidays: Morgat, Baden Baden, Minorca. Bad ones: Beg Miel, Sardinia.

Yateley was so quiet when we went there, a mere village. I loved to escape from the hurly-burly of the racecourse and watch the cricket at Wellington in an atmosphere of complete peace. The clock there had a chime that seemed to take me back to my own childhood.

Builders: By far the best we had was Mr Batt who unfortunately died of a heart attack.

Neighbours can be very trying but we had no cause ever to complain about the Colls family, always friendly and hospitable, never intrusive. I caught rather a bad cold twice at their annual Christmas fireworks party.

Everyday recollections: Walking with Turpin to the post office and invariably passing 'the nodder' on the way.

Uncouth recollection: being kissed on the ear by Anthea Dingwall in Tices the grocers.

Embarrassing recollection: Making a speech at Mary-Rose Dingwall's wedding to a plump and rather odious young man.

Happy recollections: Picnics at the 'Robbers Cave' and races afterwards, getting the car stuck on Charles's birthday, my mother at her nicest on the day Louise was christened, Charles always modest, hanging a towel over the window before taking a plunge in the downstairs bathroom, tea with Gus Dalrymple of the Sporting Life.

Horticultural successes: dahlias, tomatoes and huge, quite uneatable vegetable marrows. In our early days I used to take garden produce to London (I had to go to the office on Sundays) and flog it to the de Wesselows and Surtees. The little bit of extra money meant quite a lot.

Day of slight pride: Charles passing the Common Entrance exam into Eton.

Surprises: Jane, aged nine, handing me a written ultimatum on Christmas afternoon, including no more family walks.

As my recollections of the earlier days at Yateley, perhaps the best days, are getting hazy I shall stop here and hand what I have written over to Charles.

Acknowledgements

Huge thanks to my excellent editor Andreas Campomar, who edited *Dear Lupin* and whose idea this was. Also big thanks to my other half Tim and my younger sister Lumpy for their unstinting support.